Dyer Daniel Lum

Social Problems of Today

The Mormon Question in its Economic Aspects

Dyer Daniel Lum

Social Problems of Today
The Mormon Question in its Economic Aspects

ISBN/EAN: 9783337296308

Printed in Europe, USA, Canada, Australia, Japan

Cover: Foto ©Suzi / pixelio.de

More available books at **www.hansebooks.com**

SOCIAL PROBLEMS OF TO-DAY;

OR,

THE MORMON QUESTION

IN

ITS ECONOMIC ASPECTS.

A STUDY OF CO-OPERATION AND ARBITRATION IN
MORMONDOM, FROM THE STANDPOINT
OF A WAGE-WORKER.

" That's the most perfect government in which an injury to one is the concern of all."

BY A GENTILE,

AUTHOR OF "UTAH AND ITS PEOPLE."

D. D. LUM & CO., PORT JERVIS, N. Y.
1886.

CONTENTS.

———

CHAPTER I.

WHAT IS THE MORMON PROBLEM?

CÆSAR'S spirit still stalks the earth. It finds footing in the American, as it did in the Roman republic. Time has but shifted the scenes, not altered the plot, in the historic drama. Having scaled Olympus and brought the gods into unity, its imperial claims will not relax for man. Driven from the church, it sought refuge in the State; the power ecclesiasticism lost, politics gained. The danger to liberty to-day lies not in priestcraft, but in statecraft; not in the enforced obedience of the people to revealed law, but in the enforced obedience to assumed social requirements. Duties are held as individual, rights social, and the individual has to bend before the phantasmal abstraction "society." For centuries progress has been toward greater freedom; every extension of liberty has widened the sphere of personal freedom In America, legislation is apparently tending toward greater restriction. Fifty years ago many of our present legislative schemes would have been impossible. "The American Idea" of that day was—"the best government is that which governs least;' hence men looked with jealousy on encroachments on individual rights. In fact, the essence of government was supposed to be protection to individual rights, that only in the extension of personal freedom could there be social freedom. Or, as expressed by one of the revolutionary heroes, Thomas Paine:

If we are asked what government is, we hold it to be nothing more than a national association, and we hold that to be the best which secures to every man his rights, and promotes the greatest quantity of happiness with the least expense. * * * Man's natural rights are the foundation of all his civil rights.

Why this eddy in the stream of progress; this apparent drift to force and "strong government;" this rejuvenance of Cæsar's ghost, urging centralization and reliance on might?

The answer is plainly to be seen. The spirit of Cæsar, rendered powerless in religious systems, castrated of divine right in forms of political government, is entrenching itself in the economic system of the age. British and German empires, Spanish and Italian kingdoms, French and American republics, are but dead forms, survivals of past political conditions; the animating soul in each is the same. A common (economic) feeling has made them all akin. The burgher class has mounted the throne, and cries halt to progress. Statecraft exists, to-day, for the furtherance of economic interests; *forms* of government are recognized as of secondary importance to "vested interests" and commercial *rights*. Harrington's apophthegm: "Empire follows the balance of property," is no longer disputable.

In the opening of the Slavery discussion, between North and South, we trace the beginning of the inevitable conflict now upon us. The North, as representative of our transitional *régime*, demanded room. In the way of the extension of *cheap* labor stood the dear labor of slavery. The struggle between the manufacturer and the importer, dignified as "the tariff question," gave way to a deeper problem. The non-extension of slavery into the territories was not a sentimental issue, but an economic one. The manufacturing and farming class instinctively felt that their existence depended upon the result. To secure the extension of the blessings of an abstract freedom, to restrict slave labor and confine it within defined bounds, all was permissible. "The end justifies the means." Hence, in the name of *freedom* the construction of the constitution was twisted into the furtherance of *power*. Our fathers ate sour grapes, and we wonder that our teeth are set on edge. The anti-slavery sentiment gave the government power to secure ideal freedom and actual centralization. The North, true to the ideal, rushed to the front and established, with the non-extension and final extinction of slavery, the extension and permanence of *cheap* labor! And for this we display our wounds!

The precedents thus formed, the forced grafts on the constitution (logically necessary), and the exigencies of our alleged commercial competition, form the justification of the "Edmunds" anti-polygamy law. Having entered upon the path of coercion, we are powerless to halt; in fact, each year increases the tendency and augments the momentum in that direction. Republican rule has shaped our history; Democracy can but administer on the legacy bequeathed.

The whole Mormon system, social, religious, industrial, is essentially based on two fundamental principles: *coöperation* in business and *arbitration* in disputes. Necessarily, in the eyes of monopoly-restricted competition, this is a foe. It could be faced by no more deadly enemy. If this be true, and the following pages will contain the proof, we need not wonder that an effort should be made "to fire the popular heart," and excite animosity against a people so hostile to feeing lawyers and the cent. per cent. policy of our commercial lords. The old cry for *freedom* through increase of central *power*—the anti-slavery justification—cannot well be urged again; hence the moral standard is unfurled. Monogamy (with its "twin relic" Prostitution) is no more a question in the minds of the worshippers at the shrine of the commonplace, who draw official salaries in Utah, than Catholicism to the mind of Charles V. It is but an excuse for ulterior ends; a means to increase power and reap the fruit of extortion. No man doubted a few centuries ago the right to use force to attain Catholic unity, unless his mind was tainted with heretical doctrines. Philip II. of Spain, and Elizabeth of England, were in hearty unison on suppressing opinion in the interest of the State. But to-day the only heresy recognized by the State is that of the marital relation; here it differs from the traditional mode. So no man can to-day assert that monogamy is but an article of belief, a private *credo*, but lo! he is branded as a defender of polygamy or promiscuity.

But we need not waste words on polygamy, though the Utah system is well worth study. *That is not the issue!* That is but the gaudily-colored bait to catch the inexperienced denizens of economic waters. The issue is again an economic one—the extension of cheap labor—the cent. per cent. freedom of commercial intercourse—the control over the means of life of the many by the few, confronted in Utah by an antagonistic system of social and commercial activity.

To all who believe that Co-operation and Arbitration are the key notes of a higher civilization, that they are only means by which we may be saved from "shooting Niagara" as a nation, the study of the "Mormon question" is one of imperative interest. The writer served three years to establish centralization of power at Washington, and the extension of free trade in labor at the South, under the glamour of the cry of freedom. Other fools stand ready to obey the behests of Cæsar's spirit, if need be, to again make the Republic the pathway to an Empire, their alleged minds lit by the *ignis fatuus* of *social* morality. The Mormon protest is one of deep significance to working men and women. The Eastern demand is that of Cæsar. The despised Mormon is an unconscious ally in what is not as yet a Lost Cause. As such let us endeavor to understand his position, to put ourselves in his place, before forging weapons for his opponents which will react upon us. Before giving assent to new Coercion Acts now before Congress, let us endeavor to understand Mormondom as it exists under present legislation, the spirit of the people, their institutions, and whether we are concerned in their preservation.

CHAPTER II.

CO-OPERATION.

THE exorbitant charges to which travelers in the far West are generally subjected, is a matter well known. Mormon territory is the only place west of the Rocky Mountains where there has been a systematic effort to remedy this evil. In California the growth of population has led to the diminution of prices and the restoration of the economical balance with that of the Atlantic coast; but the reform has been effected in Utah by other means. Although fair competition is fully recognized as the governing principle in trade, the remedy was projected before the growth of population rendered competition an available solution. The growth of the community had been slow and under extreme difficulties. Driven out of Ohio, Missouri and Illinois by the fanatical hatred of the mob, before polygamy was a cardinal feature in their social life, they had undertaken the hazardous task of crossing the vast alkaline plains of the great West, in hopes that in some far distant spot their wives and little ones might be free from Christian intolerance and midnight marauders. Entering the Salt Lake Valley on July 24, 1847, on what was then foreign soil and a barren desert far from civilization, they proposed to settle. There was no settlement of white men near, and they found but a few naked Indians making a meal from roasted crickets and dried grasshoppers. The few trappers they met *en route* laughed at the idea of a colony subsisting in such a region, and expressed grave doubts whether grain would mature. The once famous mountaineer, James Bridger, was so certain that failure alone was possible, that he offered to give a thousand dollars for the first ear of corn raised in the valley. Nature had limited their choice of location to places where water was accessible. On the south were extensive cactus plains; on the East the barren rocks of the Wahsatch range; on the west the great saline desert, while to the north were the volcanic lands extending down from Idaho. Irrigation had never been tried on this continent on an extensive scale, and yet without it starvation awaited them. In united action, and the holding of water as public property, lay their salvation as a community; and the interminable disputes which have arisen and the claims advanced by outsiders, actuated by private greed, have naturally tended to extend co-operation beyond the matter of irrigation. But it is not alone to natural environment that Mormon cooperation arose, for from the earliest epoch of the church Joseph Smith had made it the bulwark of the nascent church. In his eyes it was the means by which a universal social redemption was to be brought about. Fifty years ago Mormon preachers insisted that without social redemption, the millennial reign was impossible. In that early day was organized the "Order of Enoch," and it signified simply the inauguration of a society based upon a perfect co-operative order where there were to be "no poor in Zion." This was the grand aim of Joseph Smith, and co-operation is as much a cardinal and essential doctrine of the Mormon church as baptism for the remission of sins, and every Mormon elder who understands the philosophy of his own system will affirm that without co-operation salvation remains but a dream.

They entered Utah imbued with this conviction; with confident faith they sought to wrest from Nature one of her most desolate and forbidding regions. Those dreary wastes of alkaline plains and sage-brush under their efforts have given place to blooming orchards and fields of golden grain; the wigwam has been supplanted by cottages embowered in green foliage, and by thriving villages and cities.

I am frank to say that I do not believe that this conquest could have been wrested from Nature by individual efforts, by settlers isolated from each other, without mutual aid and assistance; nor that this mutual aid, under such circumstances, would have been extended but for the religious bond which knit the pioneers into a common brotherhood. The obstacles to overcome were too great; nature presented too forbidding an aspect to permit of this great conquest having resulted from the unorganized and undirected labors of isolated settlers. It was a warfare upon Nature by drilled cohorts, animated by a common feeling, and therefore, accomplished what guerilla warfare would have been incapable of achieving. There was needed the unifying element of a deep moral conviction, nerving men's souls to withstand difficulties and welding individual interests together to form closer social ties.

We give credit for sincerity to the bigoted Puritans, to the exiled Huguenots, to the followers of that (truly) Catholic Lord Baltimore, when they sought to found homes on this continent; but, for men who in face of far greater difficulties, and having passed through a persecution equally as relentless as any from which our forefathers fled, we are too often content to shrug our shoulders, and with a sneer say, *superstition.* Thirty-five years ago the co-operative social gospel of the Mormons attracted the attention and won the admiration of such socialistic apostles of England as Robert Owen, George Jacob Holyoake, and Bronterre O'Brien, the latter of whom said that the Mormons had "created a soul under the ribs of death."

Such united action and cordial co-operation, in such an emergency as their advent in Utah, shows that there must have been a master mind among them, who not only possessed their confidence, but was entitled to it by the wisdom of his counsel. That such a man was Brigham Young I think is now the impartial verdict of history. From the very first, Brigham Young "set his face as a flint" against the selfish spirit of avarice governing trade under which Mormon and Gentile alike groaned, yet he has been charged with fostering that which he essentially modified. Whatever may be our opinion of his faith, however much we may dissent from his religious views, it is impossible for any intelligent man to stand beside the simple slab which lies over his final resting-place, and not to feel that there lies a man whose worthiest monument exists in the hearts of people he led, and in the living institutions his indefatigable zeal did so much to establish. Long years before co-operation became an established principle in mercantile affairs, he tried to induce the leading merchants to inaugurate a co-operative distributive system by which the necessities of life would be cheapened and the people reap the benefit. Merchants were making enormous profits. Wheat, for instance, was bought for seventy-five cents a bushel and sold in the mining camps for twenty-five dollars per hundredweight. At last a leading firm apostatized, and the channels of trade were being used against social interests. In 1856 there was a famine in Utah, and the community was barely preserved by the leading men wisely rationing the whole and dividing among the people their own substance. Utah in her early days was utterly destitute of *cash;* all her internal trade being conducted by barter and the due bill system. In 1864 merchants had risen to opulence. Commerce was gradually, but surely, throwing all the money to a few hands. What had been so long preached as theory, had to be realized in practice or to abandon settled convictions. It had become a question of social preservation against selfish interests. Early in 1868, the merchants were startled by the announcement "that it was advisable that the *people* of Utah Territory should become their own merchants;" and that an organization should be created for them expressly for importing and distributing merchandize on a comprehensive plan. Although in the prosecution of this work the church was threatened with a formidable schism, Brigham Young never faltered; it was an economic rather than a religious heresy he had to confront. In Mormon society, the two elements of organization—the social and the religious—have ever been combined, and it was to prevent their threatened divorce that this step became necessary.

In October, 1868, President Young called a meeting of the merchants, and it was then and there determined to adopt a general co-operative plan throughout the Territory. The late Mr. Jennings, one of the largest merchants and perhaps one of the wealthiest men in Utah, rented his store to a co-operative association for five years. The people possessed the genius of co-operation and Brigham Young possessed the *will;* while around him there was a small circle of men who, for commercial energy and honor, instincts for great enterprises, and financial capacity generally, would be esteemed as pre-eminent in any commercial emporium in the world. The policy which had been wisely and considerately pursued in purchasing the stocks of existing firms, or receiving them as investments at just rates, shielded from embarrassment those who otherwise would have inevitably suffered from the inauguration and prestige of the new organization. Simultaneously with the framing of the parent institution, local organizations were formed in most of the settlements of the Territory; each drawing their supplies mainly from the one central depot. The people, with great unanimity, became shareholders in their respective local "co-op's," and also in the parent institution, "Zion's Co-operative Mercantile Institution." Thus, almost in a day, was effected a great reconstruction of the commercial relations and methods of an entire community, which fitted the purposes of the times and preserved the temporal unity of the Mormon people, as well as creating for them a mighty financial bulwark.

In Brigham Young's suggestions for great things he never forgot the small; industrial independence was the constant star that illuminated his horizon. To build mills, establish factories, to reclaim the desert, to gather the poor, to provide labor, to show a novice how to carve out a living from rugged nature, were as strongly marked characteristics of his life as his *rôle* as a religious teacher. While in fact founding a state, he in detail encouraged industry and the use of all natural resources which best subserved self-sustenance and independence and the multiplication of peaceful and happy homes. Men of narrower views surrounded him, men who, however strong in religious convictions, deemed the laws of trade as practically paramount to the golden rule of equity, and the acquisition of a dollar the one chief end of man.   It was uphill work for him among even his own people who had tasted of the fruit of greed; and too often acquiescence from religious considerations lacked that warmth and force which comes of genuine activity and some sacrifice for others' welfare.   Disappointment, mortification and chagrin were powerless to weaken his determination, though backwardness to comprehend, faltering by the way from self-interest, the ready forgetfulness and the flagging interest in things that led from personal profit, must have sorely tried his indomitable will.   Yet probably the historian will not question this discipline to which he was subjected, for we may think that a more abundant success would have ministered to personal egotism and made him still more imperious than he was wont to be.

The hard facts of history point to uncommon sacrifice, to self-abnegation, to the yielding of personal will and individual preference in deference to counsel and in opposition to any prospective personal advantage.   Mineral in the soil, crickets in the field, water in limited quantity and often a long way off; timber in almost inaccessible places, saw-mills of the most primitive character, winters of startling severity under the circumstances, with many necessities and all luxuries a thousand miles away; no money, no market, no mines, nothing save the free air, the solemn snow-capped mountains, the parched prairie, and the dust and powder of desert lands.   The power of irrigation was untried and unknown, seed was scarce, meat anything but abundant; stores had slowly risen and instituted exchange by barter; all the circumstances and the natural surroundings tended to call into play the selfish instincts of man's nature in the supreme struggle for existence.   Yet amid this people, with clothing worn out, shoeless, hatless, and coatless, the ragged and rugged Pioneers heard, in undisguised amazement, the calm assertion that in Salt Lake City wearing apparel should be offered in abundance at prices discounting those of New York !

The heaviest concern in Utah is Zion's Co-operative Mercantile Institution, of Salt Lake City; which, with its branches in Logan, Ogden and Provo, imports one third of all the merchandize in the Territory. It has a cash capital of $1,000,000.   This institution, with the aid of the local co-operative stores in the villages which it supplies, have succeeded in bringing down prices to within the reach of the poorest, being patronized by all classes.   The community is no longer at the mercy of a few traders, nor can scarcity increase prices: the necessities of the people can no longer be taken advantage of and immense profits made by adventurers whose only aim is to amass a fortune. The money of the citizens, instead of going out of the Territory, remains to build up and encourage home industries. Stockholders in the various co operative associations in Utah may be counted by the thousands. So we may say, that co-operation has been raised from a religious duty to a voluntary and profitable system, and presented on a grander scale than any where else in the world.

I have before me the two semi-annual reports of the Z. C. M. I. for the fiscal year ending October 5, 1885. The following extracts will convey a very fair idea of the condition of the Institution and the amount of business done.

From the report of the first half of the fiscal year:

* * * So far as the financial condition of the Institution is concerned, we have abundant cause for thankfulness. For while our sales, in consequence of the general dullness experienced throughout the country, have fallen somewhat below what they were a year ago, yet I find they have been all we reasonably could expect.

The stocks of merchandize on hand, as shown in our inventories, are valued at $1,144,960.81, which is $119,791.05 less than we carried one year ago. I find that nearly 79 per cent. of this merchandize on hand has been paid for. Included in the merchandize on hand, as given above, are the following home-made goods: Boots and shoes, $49,543.42; Provo woolen goods, $49.325.67; soaps, brooms, trunks, crackers, candy and matches, $4,680. Total home-produced articles, $103,549.09.

Our merchandize and cash on hand aggregate $1,189,192.78, or over 65 per cent. more than the sum total of all our liabilities, of course exclusive of capital stock and reserve fund.

For freight and express charges, we have paid for the half year, $137,784.94, and our sales have been about $1,700,000. Cash receipts for the half year have been $1,775,719.76.

An accurate inventory of the material, machinery, and tools has been taken in the manufacturing depots, and I am gratified in being able to say the results are very satisfactory. In the shoe factory, there were turned out 11,590 pairs of boots, and 80,465 pairs of shoes, at a cost of $148,514.12. The tannery used 4,362 hides, 1,157 skins, and produced $53,007 worth of sole leather, buff, wax upper, calf and kip skins. At our clothing factory $50,493.51 worth of clothing was manufactured, consisting of some 30 different kinds of garments, including overalls, of which there were 60,900 pairs turned out. The total product of these three manufacturing departments is valued at $252,014.77, and they give employment to nearly two hundred operatives of one grade or another.

The following statement of assets and liabilities shows the condition of the institution at the close of the fiscal half year:

RESOURCES.

Mdse. on hand...............................	$1,444,960.81
Notes receivable.............................	244,667.26
Accounts receivable..........................	253,187.41
Cash on hand................................	44,231.97
Real estate in Salt Lake City, Ogden, Logan, Soda Sp'gs and Provo...........................	231,722.59
Machinery at Shoe and Clothing Factories and tann'ry	33,220.32
17 horses, 2 mules, 16 wagons, 10 sets of harness, 10 tons of oats, and 4 tons of hay...............	2,756.00
Provo Manuf. Stock..........................	272.65
	$1,955,019.01

LIABILITIES.

Bills payable.................................	$570,032.29
Accounts payable.............................	68,503.53
Provo Manuf. Com'y and others for commission goods	75.051.61
Unpaid dividends.............................	3,035.34
Temporary deposits by customers..............	1,411.89
Outstanding orders drawn on us for mdze. at retail....	1,488.54
Capital stock................................	999,995.32
Reserves	171,186.57
Undivided profits............................	64,313.92
	$1,955,019.01

A dividend was declared of 5 per cent. upon the capital stock, which will take of the undivided profits $49,999.80, and the balance will be credited to the reserve fund.

At the second meeting—held in October 1885, another dividend of five per cent. was declared, and the report showed the institution to be in a flourishing condition, the business done during the preceding six months being somewhat in excess of that of the first half of the fiscal year, with excellent prospects ahead. The following extracts are suggestive:

Our indebtedness for merchandize purchased is less to-day than it has been for many years past, and our condition generally is sound and satisfactory.

During the half year we have disposed of some seventy thousand (70,000) bushels of our Cache Valley wheat at figures that, although not giving large margins of profit, paid us for our trouble and were satisfactory. We have also succeeded in marketing many car-loads of other produce, such as eggs, butter, oats, barley, etc , from that section, at figures that left us a small margin after expenses were paid.

From Utah, Sanpete and Tooele valleys we have moved a number of cars of wheat, oats and flour, and although no direct profit was made for the Institution by the transaction, yet we were indirectly benefited in being able to turn this produce into money which helped to liquidate debts on our books.

An examination of this report will show that production as well as distribution enters into the policy of Utah coöperation. The Z. C. M. I., feeling the necessity of home production, has started factories in several articles of production. They bought out the machinery and part of the stock of the Boot and Shoe Factory known as the "Working Men's Co-operative Association." The Deseret Tannery Association, with which a shoe factory in connection was contemplated, finally merged into the Z. C. M. I., that institution holding in its hands much of the trade of the Territory, and possessing unequaled facilities for distribution. From that moment to the present, without a solitary drawback, and in spite of many obstacles, the increased demand and manufacture have run parallel with each other. In December, 1884, there were some 150 employed in producing about 400 pairs of shoes or boots per day, in every variety and style and fashion.

From a letter from the Z. C. M. I., I extract the following as of interest to the reader:

SALT LAKE CITY, UTAH.
May 28th, 1886.

*   *   *   *   *   *   *   *

Our annual sales are nearly 5,000,000. The building we occupy in this city is four stories in height, 318 feet in length and 100 feet in width. We employ in this building about 125 persons; our Shoe Factory, Tannery and Clothing Factory, also in this city, give employment to about 275 men, women and girls. For the purpose of supplying the residents of the Territory with a pure article of drugs and medicines, we started what is known as our Drug Department, where we keep pure and reliable articles; and in this way, guard our patrons from the impositions of quacks. Our business is flourishing and is increasing each month. For the present month, I presume our sales will aggregate at least \$14,000 more than they did for the corresponding period of last year. It is rare that we have to sue for a debt. I think I may safely say that no more than half a dozen instances can be enumerated where the Institution has been the plaintiff in suits to recover a debt. We are careful and judicious in our credits, and in a few instances where local co-operative stores have through accident, misfortune, or bad management run very much behind, we have called their stockholders together, discussed the situation with them, and have convinced them that all they needed was a vigorous effort and they could soon place themselves on a sure and solid footing; that to accomplish this desirable purpose we would take a note for their total indebtedness to us, said note bearing a low rate of interest. We would then encourage them to organize their little stores, put more capital into them and purchase their goods from us for cash. By so doing they in all instances realized from the cash discounts that we gave them more than enough to pay the interest of the old debt, and gradually as they again accumulated means, a portion of it from time to time was applied on the old debt; and in this way after a series of years all was cleared off, and their transactions with us from that time henceforth were for cash, and we think no inducement could be held out to them to go to the old long credit system.

As a people you are aware that we do not believe in law suits. We prefer to settle our difficulties by arbitration, believing fully that it saves a vast amount of bad feeling between people who should be friends, and should study each other's interest; by this a large saving is made in lawyer's fees and court expenses.

I am, yours truly,
H. S. ELDREDGE, Supt.

One feature of interest to every buyer is this, that net cost of manufacture only is charged up to the Institution, so that but one profit—and that a small one—is between the producer and the consumer. But it is unnecessary to illustrate further. That co-operation has succeeded in supplanting personal stores and factories, I do not assert, but rather that co-operation is the defined policy of Mormon society. Some extracts from representative sources will clearly establish this fact. From the *Z. C. M. I. Advocate*, for March 15th, 1886, I quote the following as an official statement of the views of their directors:

The best exponent of co-operation is Z. C. M. I., of course, not perfect by any means, not as fully co-operative as it could be made, not owned and held strictly by the majority of the people in all sections of the Territory, but, yet despite of whatever restrictions it may have been subjected to, it has ever been the undeviating friend of the people, its authorities have studied the public good, and its stockholders have been satisfied with what might be considered a moderate dividend on their investment; it has set an example in this respect, and the community would have been more protected, and received greater advantages, had the same spirit directed all the local co-operative stores, of the Territory. There are numbers of prosperous stores and there are far more dragging out a lingering existence, in the several settlements, but every one could be absorbed and the profits—if any—inure to the people, if ostensible co-operative stores were properly conducted and popularly patronized.

The great drawback of narrowed co-operative, as of combined or personal stores, is, that the primary object is to make money. It is not a percentage simply on the investment that is expected or desired, big profits and fortune is the ultimatum; and the closer we come to co-operation, if this selfish spirit prevails, the greater the evil, for the assumption and presumption is, that such store or organization possesses a claim upon the town or settlement, and so if illy regulated it becomes a monopoly as grasping and avaricious as the most exacting could desire. Is it not because of this that so-called co-op's have lost prestige and that in little towns where one jealously guarded store would have been ample for necessity, there are now from ten to twenty, dividing the interests, feelings, and working against the progress of the body temporal in almost every sense?

Interesting as an account of co-operative enterprises in Utah may be, it must give way to the great manifestoes of the church upon her social and co-operative systems. The following Encyclical Letter, or apostolic circular, is probably unique in its character among church documents, and as it shows so clearly the spirit of the leaders of the so-called Theocracy, I shall make liberal extracts. It is said to be from the pen of George Q. Cannon, and bears date July 10th, 1875. A careful perusal will throw more light upon the "Mormon Problem" than a study of all the congressional harangues made on the subject. Here are its main points:

To the Latter-day Saints:—

The experience of mankind has shown that the people of communities and nations among whom wealth is the most equally distributed, enjoy the largest degree of liberty, are the least exposed to tyranny and oppression, and suffer the least from luxurious habits which beget vice. * * *

One of the great evils with which our own nation is menaced at the present time is the wonderful growth of wealth in the hands of a comparatively few individuals. The very liberties for which our fathers contended so steadfastly and courageously, and which they bequeathed to us as a priceless legacy, are endangered by the monstrous power which this accumulation of wealth gives to a few individuals and a few powerful corporations. By its seductive influence results are accomplished which, were it more equally distributed, would be impossible under our form of government. It threatens to give shape to the legislation, both State and National, of the entire country. If this evil should not be checked, and measures not be taken to prevent the continued enormous growth of riches among the class already rich, and the painful increase of destitution and want among the poor, the nation is liable to be overtaken by disaster; for, according to history, such a tendency among nations once powerful was the sure precursor of ruin. The evidence of the restiveness of the people under this condition of affairs in our times is witnessed in the formation of societies of grangers, of patrons of husbandry, trades' unions, etc., etc., combinations of the productive and working classes against capital. Years ago it was perceived that we Latter-day Saints were open to the same dangers as those which beset the rest of the world. A condition of affairs existed among us which was favorable to the growth of riches in the hands of a few at the expense of the many. A wealthy class was being rapidly formed in our midst whose interests, in the course of time, were likely to be diverse from those of the rest of the community. The

2

growth of such a class was dangerous to our union; and, of all people, we stand most in need of union and to have our interests identical. Then it was that the Saints were counseled to enter into co-operation. In the absence of the necessary faith to enter upon a more perfect order revealed by the Lord unto the church, this was felt to be the best means of drawing us together and making us one. Zion's Co-operative Mercantile Institution was organized, and, throughout the Territory, the mercantile business of the various wards and settlements was organized after that pattern. Not only was the mercantile business thus organized, but at various places branches of mechanical, manufacturing, and other productive industries were established upon this basis. To-day, therefore, co-operation among us is no untried experiment; it has been tested, and whenever fairly tested, and under proper management, its results have been most gratifying and fully equal to all that was expected of it, though many attempts have been made to disparage and decry it, to destroy the confidence of the people in it and have it prove a failure. From the day that Zion's Co-operative Mercantile Institution was organized until this day it has had formidable and combined opposition to contend with, and the most base and unscrupulous methods have been adopted by those who have no interest for the welfare of the people, to destroy its credit. Without alluding to the private assaults upon its credit which have been made by those who felt that it was in their way and who wished to ruin it, the perusal alone of the telegraphic dispatches and correspondence to newspapers, which became public, would exhibit how unparalleled in the history of mercantile enterprises has been the hostility it had to encounter. That it has lived, notwithstanding these bitter and malignant attacks upon it and its credit, is one of the most valuable proofs of the practical worth of co operation to us as a people. Up to this day Z. C. M. I., has had no note go to protest; no firm, by dealing with it, has ever lost a dollar; its business transactions have been satis-factory to its creditors, and yet its purchases have amounted to fif-teen millions of dollars ! What firm in all this broad land can point to a brighter or more honorable record than this ? * * *

It was not for the purpose alone, however, of making money that Z. C. M. I. was established. A higher object than this prompted its organization. A union of interests was sought to be attained. At the time co-operation was entered upon, the Latter-day Saints were acting in utter disregard of the principles of self-preservation. They were encouraging the growth of evils in their own midst which they condemned as the worst features from which they had been gathered. Large profits were being concentrated in comparatively few hands, instead of being generally distributed among the people. As a consequence, the community was being rapidly divided into classes, and the hateful and unhappy distinctions which the pos-session and lack of wealth give rise to, were becoming painfully apparent. When the proposition to organize Z. C. M. I., was broached, it was hoped that the community at large would become its stockholders; for if a few individuals only were to own its stock, the advantages to the community would be limited. The people, therefore, were urged to take shares, and large numbers responded to the appeal. As we have shown, the business proved as successful as its most sanguine friends anticipated. But the distribution of profits among the community was not the only benefit conferred by the organization of co-operation among us. The public at large who did not buy at its stores derived profits, in that the old practice of dealing which prompted traders to increase the price of an article because of its scarcity, was abandoned. Z. C. M. I. declined to be a party to making a corner upon any article of merchandize because of the limited supply in the market. From its organization until the present it has never advanced the price of any article because of its scarcity. Goods therefore in this Territory have been sold at something like fixed rates and reasonable profits since the Institution has had an existence, and practices which are deemed legitimate in some parts of the trading world, and by which, in this Territory, the necessities of consumers were taken advantage of— as, for instance, the selling of sugar at a dollar a pound, and domestics, coffee, tobacco and other articles at an enormous advance over original cost because of their scarcity here—have not been indulged in. In this result the purchasers of goods who have been opposed to co-operation have shared equally with its patrons.

We appeal to the experience of every old settler in this Territory for the truth of what is here stated. They must vividly remember that goods were sold here at prices which the necessities of the people compelled them to pay, and not at cost and transportation, with the addition of a reasonable profit. The railroad, it is true, has made great changes in our method of doing business. But let a blockade occur, and the supply of some necessary article be very limited in our market, can we suppose that traders have so changed in the lapse of a few years that, if there were no check upon them, they would not put up the price of that article in proportion as the necessities of the people made it desirable? They would be untrue to all the training and traditions of their craft if they did not. *And it is because this craft is in danger that such an outcry is made against co-operation.* Can any one wonder that it should be so, when he remembers that, from the days of Demetrius who made silver shrines for the goddess Diana at Ephesus down to our own times, members of crafts have made constant war upon innovations that were likely to injure their business?

* * * * * * * *

Your Brethren,

BRIGHAM YOUNG,	CHARLES C. RICH,
GEORGE A. SMITH,	LORENZO SNOW,
DANIEL H. WELLS,	FRANKLIN D. RICHARDS,
JOHN TAYLOR,	GEORGE Q. CANNON,
WILFORD WOODRUFF,	BRIGHAM YOUNG, Jun.
ORSON HYDE,	ALBERT CARRINGTON."

John Taylor, the successor of Brigham Young, has been at all times as explicit and zealous in this matter as his predecessor. At the annual April Conference in 1878, he spoke in these words:

If we manufacture cloths and boots and shoes, or anything else, we want the institutions to dispose of our goods. If we need encouragement in regard to the introduction of any manufactures of any kind, we want them to help us, and we have a right to expect this of them so far as is wise, prudent and legitimate. I will state that the directors of Z. C. M. I. feel interested in the very things that I am talking about, and I say it to their credit and for your satisfaction. I do not think there is an institution in the United States in a better condition than that is to-day; and it is improving all the time, not after any fictitious manner, but on a solid, firm, reliable basis. Now then, I have proposed to these brethren, which they quite coincide with, that when they shall be able to pay a certain amount as dividends on the means invested, after reserving a sufficient amount to preserve the institution *intact* against any sudden emergency which may arise, which is proper among all wise and intelligent men, that then the profits of the institution outside of this should be appropriated for the development of home manufactures, the making of machinery, the introduction of self-sustaining principles, and the building up of the Territory generally; and they acquiesced in this feeling; and I say it to their honor and credit. And I will tell you again that the Church has got a large interest in that institution, consequently we wish to see everything go right, not on any wild, erratic principle, but on a solid, firm, reliable basis, that which when carried out will elicit the admiration and confidence of all good and honorable men.

Later, in the fiftieth annual Conference, April, 1880, "the Year of Jubilee," we find the same subject strongly insisted upon, I make the following extracts:

Elder Franklin D. Richards said:

What better can we do, in this our year of jubilee, in token of our gratitude to God for the abundance of his favors bestowed upon us, than to do good to each other, and to make glad the hearts of the poor in Israel? The authorities of the Church are thinking of doing something by way of aiding such as are needy. The officers of the Perpetual Emigration Fund Company calculate to relieve in part the worthy poor, who are owing for their emigration; and as President Taylor suggested in public on Sunday, let us all do something to aid the poor and make the hearts of the Saints rejoice, and see that no one is allowed to suffer. This same charitable feeling should extend through all our Co-operative Institutions; our rich brethren merchants who have got debts owing to them by the worthy poor, who are struggling with adversity in the world for subsistence, let them get out their accounts and send them receipted, either in full or in part to their debtors, as the case may be, with a note of forgiveness, telling them to lift up their heads and rejoice, and the

Lord will bless them for it. Let the rich men in our Territory, who have been blessed to accumulate means, and who hold notes drawing interest against their poor brethren, look over their papers, and when they find a note given by their poor but worthy brother, who has perhaps mortgaged his home and is in danger of being sold out, let them forgive the debt, and thus our rich brethren may help fulfil the prophecy that the poor shall rejoice in the Holy One of Israel. There are those who have borrowed money, and whose homes stand pledged for payment thereof, who have incurred debt through misfortune, or hard times, or perhaps through sickness, and who deserve relief—I would say to all the brethren who may be creditors of such persons, go to and make yourselves their benefactors, and establish the principle in the hearts of God's people—"Make to yourselves friends with the mammon of unrighteousness, that, when ye fail, they may receive you into everlasting habitations."

Reader, are you accustomed to such sermons? Would you not rather your mortgage rested in the hands of a Mormon Elder, than in that of an Eastern Christian? Let us be honest! On the same occasion Elder Erastus Snow announced that the books of the Company showed that the indebtedness from those who have been brought to Utah during the past thirty years, amounted to $1,600,000. And he added:

Now, it is contemplated that this year of jubilee shall be made a year of release and comfort to those who are indebted to the Fund, who have striven to do their duty and discharged it as far as able to do so, but whose circumstances have been adverse, preventing them from doing as their hearts listed.

President Taylor again spoke, announcing the decision to remit the indebtedness of "the worthy poor." And further, to remit one half due on tithing. He said:

The amount that is behind (on tithing) according to the bishop's records—which many of the people owing it signify their willingness to pay but are not able to—is $151,798. We propose releasing half of the amount to the deserving poor, and that will be $75,899. * *

Another thing. We have had a great scarcity of water the last year, and consequently short crops. It is proposed that, inasmuch as there may be suffering more or less in some places, we hope, however, that our brethren will not allow our poor unfortunate brethren to suffer. I have not heard of anything of the kind; but still a little help will not do any harm. And where people have been in straitened circumstances through the loss of crops and of stock—and some people have lost perhaps their last cow, and some have lost many of their stock, and yet have a good many left; but there has been quite a general loss. Now, we propose to raise 1000 head of cows—not old cows that do not give any milk; nor any one-teated cows, but good milk cows, and have them distributed among those that may be destitute in the different stakes, under the direction of the authorities thereof.   And the Church will put in 300 of this 1000. I spoke to Brother Sheets and told him that we did not want any one-teated cows.   The balance of this number, namely, 700, we would like the stakes to make up.   We have been informed by the presidents that this can be easily done.   It would have been quite hard awhile ago, because we lost so many of our animals; but now it seems we can do it quite easy.   [Laughter].   It is much better to give them to the poor than to have them die, and they have not all died yet, so we may as well begin to dispose of them.   * * *

And I would like to see Z. C. M. I., and our bankers, merchants, and other creditors scratch off a few names of their debtors; and I think they feel disposed to do it; I have spoken to some of the directors of Z. C. M. I., and I find that they feel about as we do.

Surely a strange discourse to our ears ! We have seen that co-operation is not only a fundamental principle in business, but permeates their religious and social relations.   The extracts I have given were from speeches before the Edmunds law went into effect.

They indicate the constant policy pursued in Mormon society. Even the Perpetual Emigration Fund, of which we hear so much from discordant shriekers, is a purely co-operative institution.   The Company has an office in Liverpool.   When a Mormon convert on the continent begins to save money to enable him and his family to emigrate to a land where independence awaits him, he sends whatever small sums he can save to the office at Liverpool where it is placed to his credit.   When the sum amounts to the larger portion of the necessary expense to reach Utah, the Company advances the remainder.   By sending all their passengers for forty years past by one line they secure reduced rates, as well as on the railroads.

In the same spirit the " Zion's Central Board of Trade,'' with branches in every county, was organized.   In the Preamble to their Articles of Association this aim is clearly laid down.   As, like every thing else Mormon, it differs so radically from Boards of Trade in other Christian communities, I invite attention to the

PREAMBLE.

The objects of this association are: To maintain a Commercial Exchange; to promote uniformity in the customs and usages of producers, manufacturers and merchants; *to inculcate principles of justice and equity in trade;* to facilitate the speedy adjustment of business pursuits; to arrange for transportation; to seek remunerative markets for home products; to foster capital and protect labor, uniting them as friends rather than dividing them as enemies; to encourage manufacturing; to aid in placing imported articles in the hands of consumers as cheaply as possible; to acquire and disseminate valuable agricultural, manufacturing, commercial and economic information; and generally to secure to its members the benefits of co-operation in the furtherance of their legitimate pursuits, and to unite and harmonize the business relations of the Stake Board of Trade, now and hereafter to be organized throughout the Territory, with those of the Central Association.

The subject is by no means exhausted, but space forbids further citations. Enough evidence has been given to show that the Mormon community is essentially a co-operative one. The bitter feeling now being excited against them by the jealousies of land-claim jumpers, saloon and faro-table keepers, mining speculators, avaricious merchants, and religious bigots, who cordially clasp hands in a brotherhood of Crusaders, cannot but result in uniting this people more firmly in co-operative unity. While this Unholy Alliance may delay the further extension of co-operative enterprise, they cannot unsettle established results. Though united in the bonds of a common enmity, their motives are widely different. One class wishing to expropriate the fertile farms wrested from the desert by honest industry; another angered by the want of patronage at their bars or counters, and who view with selfish alarm the temperance of the people or the lessening of prices by co-operation; still another who in the spirit of greed would convert peaceful agricultural communities into lawless mining camps; while with these are joined the asinine bray of the gospel exhorter, amazed to find his appeal to flee from the wrath to come and to subscribe towards giving him a comfortable salary falling on deaf ears. As the *Z. C. M. I. Advocate* truly says:

Co-operation, unity of action, of effort and of means, will surely be the one—the only method of securing freedom from arbitrary and tyrannical rule, and from dependence on those who understand nothing, and care less, for the aspirations of the people of Utah Territory.

CHAPTER III.

ARBITRATION vs. LITIGATION.

THANKS to the publicity given to Mr. T. V. Powderly's recent letters, we have learned that a large body of working men and women are enthusiastic admirers of the principle of arbitration in matters of dispute in lieu of resorting to litigation, or the often still more expensive custom of "strikes." How far this principle is a fundamental feature in Mormon society cannot but be a matter of interest to all those who hold that arbitration is an index of higher civilization and progress. Though the word "arbitration" may not be in familiar use in Utah, we shall see that what we denote by that term has been their long-established custom.

In the first place, to more readily understand the subject, we must consider in what relation the "priesthood" stands to the people in Utah. And as it may be well to let the Mormon state the case for himself, I clip the following from the columns of the *Deseret News*, of Salt Lake City, of March 3, 1885:

Another pertinent question is often asked. Does not the practice of the tenets of your faith supersede and supplant the government in the exercise of some of its powers and functions? By no means. We have courts of arbitration which sit in civil cases to adjust difficulties and that too without compensation. The tendency is also to the reconciliation of the parties litigant, instead of the bitter hate that often follows a vexatious and expensive law suit. Let me here ask, is there any less likelihood of correct judgment being rendered by these disinterested parties, who sit as neighbors without compensation, than in courts of law? I think not. Are not important questions involving issues of the gravest consequences arbitrated, and that, too, satisfactorily to all concerned? No sound lawyer will object to this course, while a hungry pettifogger who desires to fleece his fellow-man might complain and declare there ought to be a law prohibiting the exercise of such powers. We are forbidden, however, by revelation to interfere in criminal matters. Persons guilty of such offences we are expressly enjoined to deliver up to the *law of the land*, for a person thus guilty is unworthy a place amongst us and has no claim upon any of the privileges of the Church. Further, to screen a man or woman guilty of criminality would place us under the ban of the Almighty. Let me here ask,

Would the Almighty reveal a principle that was or could rightly be interpreted to be criminal or unconstitutional? I answer, in view of the eternal consistency of His character, He could not, neither has He. Will our enemies admit this? Not now; but they will be compelled to make the admission by and by, for truth is eternal and it will eternally prevail.

The hue and cry that is raised about the priesthood dictating and controlling in all political matters is so much bosh. The unity exhibited by the people at the polls is often quoted in proof of priestly rule; whereas the facts are, we have had our discussions upon the merits of the various candidates previous to the day of election, have expressed our opinions freely, and when left in the minority have done as caucuses and conventions generally do— yielded, to make a vote unanimous. Talk about the arbitrary rule of the Priesthood; why, the lash of the scurrilous anti-" Mormon " sheet published in this city is more potent to whip into line the Gentile minority of Utah and make them dance to its music than anything that the " Mormons " could possibly conceive. For be it known, a " Mormon " cannot be cajoled or intimidated. Such a man we have no use for, neither has the Almighty. Whether the world believe it or not, we are God's free men and expect to so continue.

Is this true? We have heard much of Mormon theocracy, of the despotic powers exercised by Mormon high-priests, and have been told that the Mormon church permits or aids the struggling farmer to get established for the purpose of securing the fruits of his labor. We hear it gravely asserted that when the farmer is rejoicing in abundance and prosperity, a long bill is presented to him by the bishop, in which there is footed up every thing advanced him, from his passage money, down to a loaf of bread, or glass of milk, given to him in the hour of need; and that he is now expected to acknowledge the debt and hand himself and his savings over to the Church, and become its serf.

Who are the priests in this theocratic State? Are our Christian churches prepared to take the ground that it is dangerous for any one denomination to become numerically strong? If our Methodist brothers were successful in their missionary efforts, and could enroll proportionately as many adherents in Utah as they were enabled to do among the Government officials sent there under Presidents Grant and Hayes, would they not hail it with delight? But would affairs be better administered, or the people less priest-ridden? Let us see.

We have been told by men who are proud of their church memberships that these poor and benighted people who have been seduced from lands of Christian civilization (but which, by the way, have none the less left them " benighted ") are *priest-ridden!* There is no priesthood in the sense we generally understand that term; that is, there are no salaried ministers, or priests.   There is no body of "spiritual guides" set apart and supported by the community; there is no fund, no tax for their support.   Every intelligent man is a "priest," or Elder, and liable at any time to be called upon to speak.   Every Mormon missionary goes forth "without purse or scrip" to preach his gospel and earn his living, for a salary is never given to them.

Hon. Geo. Q. Cannon, in one of his discourses has touched upon this point, and I here quote from his remarks:

A great many people seem to think, and some who are among us act upon the thought, that because a man holds the Priesthood, and is a religious man, and practices religion, that he should not have any voice in matters that belong to civil government.   In Washington the charge has been frequently made that all the leading offices of the Territory of Utah were held by Mormon Elders, Mormon Bishops and others.   I have frequently said,in answer to this, before committees of the Senate and House, that if we did not take Mormon Elders we would have no officers, for the reason that, as a rule, every reputable man in Utah Territory, when he attains the age of majority, holds the office of an Elder, or some other office in the Priesthood.   This explanation gave a very different view to men who did not understand our organization, and whose ignorance was taken advantage of.   In the world there are a few men in religious societies, who hold leading positions, hold what we would call, if in our Church, the Priesthood, and the rest are debarred, and are mere laymen.   But it is not so with us.   The bulk of the Mormon people hold the Priesthood, and every man of repute of any age is an officer in the Church.   It is said that the members of our Legislature are men who are prominent in the Priesthood. How could it be otherwise?   If a man is energetic and has any talent he of course holds some position in the Priesthood, and he is very apt to hold some prominent place.   But does this prevent him from acting in a civil office, and from dealing justly and wisely for the good of the people?   No, we have proved to our entire satisfaction that this is not the case.

The Elders in the Mormon Church are the men who have the most intelligence and moral fitness for the position, farmers, mechanics, business men; men who have the most interest in the prosperity of the Territory.   The higher positions, as bishops, are all filled with business men, what we would call the "solid men "of the community with conservative tendencies.   When the population gather on the Sabbath in their various tabernacles, one of these, perhaps a merchant, a manufacturer, or a professional man, is called upon to address them.   Hence the essential social character of their religion, and its strong hold upon the people. An intelligent knowledge of men's wants is a pre-requisite to preferment, and the spiritual power is intelligent public opinion guarding social interests, and moral as well as material progress.

In Brooklyn, the "City of Churches," a Mormon "priest," earning his bread by his daily labor, has sent over four hundred persons to Utah, and a hundred more have gone from the shores of Long Island Sound, converted by self-supporting Mormon preachers, to find for themselves homes. Do you suppose that these men, mechanics, oyster fishermen, etc., have either materially or spiritually suffered by the change? Let us be candid.

One of the features in the Mormon Church which struck me most forcibly is its apparent democracy. Twice every year, on April 6, and October 6, the Mormons come from far and near to assemble in semi-annual Conference. Travelers relate meeting ox-teams in distant cañons headed toward "Zion," in which will be, perhaps, some lone old man or woman, with a scant stock of meal and bacon, making a one or two weeks' journey to get fresh inspiration and courage for the battle of life. At these Conferences, lasting for several days, every member has a vote; humble believer and dignitary meet on a common footing—having equal rights. At these conferences, and mark this well, every officer in the Church, including Brigham Young in his day, and John Taylor now, has to be re-elected to each and every position they hold. It may be said that this is but a mere form; that the Head of the Church is recognized as infallible and dictates his own election and that of his associates.

As long as there is perfect confidence in the First Presidency and in the Twelve we should naturally expect that their nominations would be heartily ratified. But here is a provision by which the Church itself can curb any of its officers, even to its head, whenever there is a forfeiture of public opinion by a departure from the lines laid down by usage and the collective Church. Again, in a religion alleged to be founded upon conscious imposture, where those in seats of authority are only seeking preferment and honors, where profit or ambition can alone be regarded as motives to action, how is it that there never has been a falling out among these so-called "clever rogues?"

The remissions of past indebtedness at the jubilee Conference, noticed in the last chapter were severally put to vote and carried unanimously by show of hands. On that occasion the president of the Perpetual Emigration Fund Company, in the course of his remarks, made this statement.

That reminds me of another class of Fund debtors. When I speak to them they say: "Oh, yes, we are abundantly able to pay, but you cannot collect the debt by law, because it is outlawed!" I am well aware that I cannot compel you by law to pay that indebtedness, neither would I had I it in my power; *that is not the way the Fund does its business.* All its business is conducted on the broad principle of fairness and liberality, wronging no one, benefitting everyone as far as possible.

The principle of arbitration is cardinal in the faith and practice of the Mormons; it was established and practiced long years before the same method was employed by England and America to settle the dispute over the depredations by the confederate cruisers which swept the United States merchant marine from the seas. As long ago as 1834 the principle was established in the constitution of the Mormon Church. In section 102, " Doctrines and Covenants " there is an interesting report of the organization of the High Council at Kirtland, O., February 17, 1834. This Council was to consist of the twelve Apostles and one of the three Presidents—as the case might require, and their decision is final. To obviate the difficulty of travelling long distances to settle disputes by this High Council, the Mormons have divided their numerous settlements into divisions known as Stakes, in which is established a High Council after the same pattern to accomplish the same object, viz.: to settle disputes by arbitration, having the same power—with this difference, however, that the cases tried, with evidence and decisions, are to be transmitted to the High Council of the Centre Stake, which is at present known as the Salt Lake Stake.

But before cases either civil or religious are taken to the High Council, they are tried in the Bishop's Court, composed of the Bishop and two Councilors, presiding over a "ward," or settlement, where the disputants reside; and the case is not presented in this Court till after the Teachers of the respective parties have failed to effect a reconciliation, or restitution, or satisfaction as the case might require. These various Courts of arbitration are simply ecclesiastical, and have no power to inflict punishment other than disfellowship or excommunication, according to the nature of the offence. If it is a civil suit, the offender is generally disfellowshiped till restitution is made. If it is for some violation of the moral code, such as adultery, apostacy, etc., excommunication follows. Where property has been in dispute many cases might be cited where Gentiles, familiar with the principles of justice and equity prevailing in these Mormon Courts of Arbitration, have willingly submitted their cases when a Mormon has been the litigant. As these Courts sit and act without pay, and without expense of fees for counsel, they are more likely to act on principles of exact equity.

Every "ward" has certain Teachers, whose duty it is, upon trouble arising between two Mormons, to visit them, get them to meet at some place, and, after hearing their complaints, aid them if possible to settle the difficulty by persuasion and counsel. This lower, or Teacher's Court, is composed of two members. But if no agreement is reached, then the matter is carried before the Bishop and his two Councilors, who sit as common judges and make a more searching investigation into the facts. The pro and con statements, either verbally or in writing, are made, and the testimony of the litigants and their witnesses are heard. The Court ponders the case and passes judgment. If either party is dissatisfied, he can appeal to the High Council of the Stake, to which the minutes of the Bishop's Court are transmitted, and the case comes up on its merits, or on the minutes of the Bishop's Court, as the High Council elects or determines. The High Council consists of twelve High Priests umpired by the Stake President and his Councilors. They represent respectively odd and even numbers; the odd ones on one side and the even ones on the other, the presidency in the lead. Before proceeding with the case, one, two or three "Speakers" are chosen for each side to act as special counselors or attorneys for the litigants who sit beside them. The Speakers are supposed to watch the case very closely, and have more to say during its progress than the other High Councilors; but any Councilor can speak, ask questions, etc., during the progress of the trial. If, after the decision is reached, either litigant desires to appeal to the First Presidency of the Church, he can do so, and sometimes the decisions of the lower courts are reversed by this highest tribunal, which forms its conclusions most times, though not necessarily, from the evidence contained in the minutes of the lower courts.

The following extract from the "Doctrines and Covenants" of the Church, as laid down at the formation of the first High Council, in 1834, will exhibit the spirit and method of the High Councils:

13. Whenever the Council convenes to act upon any case, the twelve Councilors shall consider whether it is a difficult one or not: if it is not two only of the Councilors shall speak upon it, according to the forms above written.

14. But if it is difficult, four shall be appointed; and if more difficult six; but in no case shall more than six be appointed to speak.

15. The accused, in all cases, has a right to one half of the Council, to prevent insult or injustice.

16. And the Councilors appointed to speak before the Council,

are to present the case after the evidence is examined in its true light before the Council, and every man is to speak according to equity and justice.

17. Those Councilors who draw even numbers, that is, 2, 4, 6, 8, 10 and 12, are the individuals who are to stand up in behalf of the accused, and prevent insult or injustice.

18. In all cases the accuser and the accused shall have the privilege of speaking for themselves before the Council after the witnesses are heard, and the Councilors who are appointed to speak in the case have finished their remarks.

All Courts are opened and closed with prayer. They generally take place in the evening, so as not to interfere with the daily avocations of the persons interested, whether members of the Court, litigants or witnesses. Each side brings his or her own witnesses, who make no charge for their attendance. Nor do either the Teachers, Bishop's Court, High Council, or First Presidency charge for their services. As illustrative of their practical working, I will quote from a letter received by the writer from a lady of high culture and attainments. She writes as follows:

May 5, 1886.

DEAR SIR: I must first apologize for the delay (unavoidable on my part) in sending you the information you desired in reference to the practice of arbitration among the Mormons, as opposed to litigation in matters of disputes between members of a community. Before touching on this subject I must remark that the great issues now at stake between Labor and Capital in the United States do not present themselves among our people. Our system of co-operation, which is carried out as far as practicable in all our home industries and enterprises, enables us to avoid the conflict between these two great social powers which at present threatens financial ruin to both. When the laborer or mechanic realizes that he is as much interested in the success of the enterprise in the prosecution of which he is a wage-earner as the capitalist who furnishes the means which render success possible, and the capitalist recognises the reciprocity of obligation existing between himself and the individual whose labor invests his gold with the power of increase, the deep, underlying cause of much of this antagonism will, I think, be removed. Co-operation, in all of its various ramifications, represents *liberty* of the individuals, *fraternity* in aim, interest and operation, and *equality* in obligation and results.

The teachings of our Church have ever condemned litigation as a means of settling differences—and the organizations of our members supply the " machinery " by which the principle of arbitration can be brought to bear practically on every question, and the right of appeal to a higher court of the same character ensures final justice and equity for all.

I will give you a case in point. A dispute arose between two individuals regarding the amount due one for labor and service. The employee claimed twenty dollars as a balance due; the employer refused to pay this amount, alleging that the services had been sufficiently remunerated when rendered, and were so acknowledged at the time by the employee. The two disputants agreed to refer the matter to the decision of the two men who acted in the capacity of *Teachers*, one belonging to each ward in which the disputants respectively lived. They met, heard the statement of the two parties, consulted together privately and decided that the employer should pay the employee five dollars, and that that sum should be a liquidation in full of all indebtedness. The employer assented, but the employee objected and appealed the matter to the Bishopric of the Ward, consisting of the Bishop and two Councilors, who compose a Bishop's court. Before these three as arbitrators the disputants presented themselves, and were permitted to bring witnesses to further establish their statements if they desired.

The parties each stated their own case, the witnesses giving their evidence, without oath or affirmation, and the arbitrators having heard all, consulted and gave their decision, which was: that the evidence offered showed that the employee had acknowledged to these parties that payment had been received according to the value at which the services were then rated, and was therefore *not entitled* to any further remuneration.

This decision was accepted by both parties, and the matter was thus settled without cost to either. An appeal might have been taken (under the laws of the Church) to a higher court, composed of fifteen members, if either party desired it, where the investigation would have been still more searching, and a larger scope of evidence admitted. In cases involving greater interests, pecuniary or otherwise, this might perhaps have been done, but the same spirit would have pervaded the entire process, *viz.*, a desire to harmonize existing differences without the antagonistic feelings so generally excited by the same. However intricate the case, or prolonged the investigation, no expense is incurred by either party, and as a general rule no publicity is given to the matter, so that the social relations of parties interested need not be disturbed by the ill-advised meddling of those perturbed spirits who are always ready to magnify trifles to the disadvantage of both parties in dispute.

I have now endeavored briefly to give you the "modus operandi" among the Latter-day Saints. Of course you understand that it is generally among our own members that this obtains. Mormons are sometimes forced into litigation by the outsiders who would not agree to any such method of settling differences, and in those cases they must defend themselves by legal process, and do not incur disapprobation by so doing.

*   *   *   *   *   *

With kind regards,
Yours respectfully,

———— ————.

The Mormons claim that their system is founded upon the following five cardinal principles, viz: Equality, Equity, Arbitration, Co-operation, and Conservatism.   As far as their system of settling disputes is concerned, I think the claim well founded.   Co-operation having awakened the animosity of the trader, we need not marvel that it should call forth denunciation from those whose whole education and life leads, for the sake of a fee, to the prostitution of intelligence to make the worse appear the better reason.

It is these councils, or " secret courts " as they are termed, that awaken the most violent opposition among the non-Mormon population in Utah.   That a people should settle differences and disputes in private, that reputable citizens should freely give their time to act as referees, and that the entire community should consequently move on harmoniously and united, fills the average mind with astonishment, and the lawyer with disgust.   And yet with such a system as has been described in the foregoing example, why should not unity of object and action prevail among the Mormons?   With the absence of litigation there is at once removed the fountain head of most of the heart-burnings, passions, and recriminations which infect social relations.   The very existence and general adoption of such a system must necessarily throw a barrier between the people and those who refuse to acknowledge it; a wall far more adamantine than mere difference in belief in creed or religious observances. Even with the elimination of polygamy, or the incarceration of the 2,000 polygamist husbands, a majority of whom became such before it had been declared illegal, there could be no hearty alliance between communities acting from such fundamentally different motives.

It is folly to charge that Mormons are driven by priestly terrorism from our civil courts to a free court of conciliation and equity in view of the above *facts*.   Beside such a method of adjusting disputes what superior advantages can our complicated system of jurisprudence offer?   The charm cannot lie in the pleasure of feeing a lawyer who offers the use of his brains to the first comer, or in popular confidence in the integrity of our judges.   Either suggestion would alike give occasion for a smile of derision.   For over fifty years this system has stood, and that it commands the confidence and respect of the Mormon people is evidenced in the fact that the records of the much vaunted superior civil courts show hardly a case of Mormon suing Mormon.   They are self-imposed and self-endured, and the uniform practice of the Mormon people sufficiently show that they meet all the requirements of social life.   To strike down Mormonism, then, is to strike down, not alone Co-operation, but the principle of Arbitration as well; and for what?   To foster a narrow selfishness in trade, to increase the power of monopoly and widen the already extended horizon of legally enforced destitution and misery. It is to strike a blow at the peace of society by supplanting the spirit of conciliation and equity with the fell spirit of discord and strife that perennially blossoms on the tree of legal litigation. Whether priestly or secular, arbitration commends itself to every candid mind, and a community in which the grasping monopolist . and the fee-seeking and strife-producing lawyer are alike ineligible to membership, is one which should awaken interest in the bosom of every intelligent producer.

While differing from the Mormons widely in their religious tenets, I will not be behind them in liberality and toleration. As a social system it has my warmest admiration, and I cordially indorse the views of a Mormon friend who writes to me in these words:

If the United States were to take pattern by the " Mormons " in these matters it would rid the country of an army of unrighteous and unjust judges, and a horde of legalized robbers known as lawyers, who feed on discussion and get rich on other people's means. If such principles as are in vogue among the " Mormons " were to prevail among the various nations, what an immense amount of treasure could be devoted to the service of the race, to say nothing of the millions of valuable lives sacrificed, to satisfy the ambition of kings and rulers, that could be saved to devote their lives to more useful pursuits. It would curtail expenses and save the taxpayers much means thrown away to prosecute legalized murder, etc.

3

CHAPTER VI.

MORALITY AND EDUCATION.

WE have seen that the Mormon community is essentially based upon co-operation in business and arbitration in differences; that the arm of the law is never invoked to settle internal disputes, although living in a country where land claims and water rights are never-failing causes of contention among their Christian neighbors. We have seen that the Church by its constitution provides for the impeachment and overthrow of their unsalaried priesthood, whenever they subordinate social requirements to private ends, and thereby lose public confidence. Confidence under these conditions can only result from merit.

A fair and considerate person, hearing a glowing description of a Mormon bishop presenting an inordinate long bill of advances made to the prosperous farmer, would be tempted to think that he must have owed his success in life to this generous aid, that his prosperity was the direct result of wisely directed social effort, and he would see nothing strange in the representative of the Church, the only organization of moral forces in the Territory, presenting the account and demanding of him, for others, like aid. Yet men who claim to be exponents of a religion professedly based on the Golden Rule call this practical illustration of their theoretical profession—tyranny! How much injustice lies in the claim we have already incidentally seen in showing the generous action of the Church in remitting one half of the indebtedness, and further that in such trials as may arise for non-payment the defendant is really before a court in equity where all are heard on their declarations of honor. The pure egotist, the grasping selfish schemer who wants to get all he can, take all if not more than is given to him, and hold all that he has, who knows nought of *duty* and insists on his *rights*, who will acknowledge no obligation not backed by legal authority, cannot understand an account appealing to a sense of duty or personal honor, and deems it a flagrant violation of his personal independence. Nor can he realize the fact that any men will give their time, without other remuneration than a sense of well-doing, for the settlement of others' disputes. But I do not propose to rest the case upon inference, or by appealing to motives and sentiments that may not be understood. Let us again appeal to the *facts.*

In the anti-polygamy law of 1862 it was provided that no church in any territory shall acquire property exceeding in value the sum of $50.000. But, it is still urged, this law could not have a retroactive effect and the Church could still hold the immense tracts already acquired. The census for 1870 gave only three estates in all Utah as exceeding 500 acres! The truth is that the whole extent of Church property, the great monopoly of land enjoyed by the Mormon theocracy, is limited to a ten-acre lot in Salt Lake City—the Temple lot. In brief, land is procured in Utah just as it is in any other Territory, and ninety-five per cent. of the Mormon population live in their own houses, on their own land, to which they hold deeds in their own names. So that if ownership of a home is one of the pre-requisites of a moral community, Utah stands well in the list.

Nor will the census of 1880 exhibit any figures to the discredit of Utah. Remembering that the tendency to increase large holdings in land has been very marked of late years, and that Utah is open to all, let us look at the census reports.

ESTATES OF 500 ACRES AND OVER IN 1880.

Territories.	Farms.	Over 500 acres.	Percentage.	Population.
Arizona	767	27	3.5	40,440
Dakota	17,435	320	1.8	135,177
Idaho	1,885	48	2.5	32,610
Montana	1,519	113	7.4	39,159
New Mexico	5,053	99	1.9	119,365
Utah	**9,452**	**45**	**.4**	**143,963**
Washington	6,529	3,100	47.7	75,116
Wyoming	457	52	11.3	20,789

When we couple this with similar statistics from the three States west of Utah, the effect of the "theocracy" upon large estates is still more marked.

ESTATES OF 500 ACRES AND OVER IN 1880.

States.	Farms.	Over 500 acres.	Percentage.	Population.
California	35,934	5,939	13.7	864,694
Nevada	1,404	281	20.+	62,266
Oregon	16,217	1,632	10.+	174,768

These figures need no comment. Self-supporting and self-reliant the Mormons have been saved from the plagues attending land monopoly, and of the few large estates given in the census, some are merely held for actual settlers, not for individual aggrandizement.

Let us now look at the subject in another phase and see whether a people exhibiting such material prosperity can be accused of illiberality and bigotry. The population of Utah, by the census of 1880, was then about 144,000, divided as follows:—

Mormons		120,283
Gentiles	14,155	
Apostate Mormons	6,988	
Josephite "	820	
Doubtful	1,716	23,680
Total		143,963

It will be seen that the "Gentiles" constitute only ten per cent. of the population, yet from this small minority are taken the incumbents of nearly every position of influence and emolument. They have the Governor, with absolute veto power, Judges, Marshals, Prosecuting Attorneys, Land Register, Recorder, Surveyor-General, Clerks of the Courts, Commissioners, Post Office, Mail Contractors, Postal Agents, Revenue Assessors and Collectors, Superintendent of Indian Affairs, Indian Agencies, Indian Supplies, Army Contractors, Associated Press Agency, and on every question affecting polygamy, all the jurors; in fact, about every territorial position not elective.

Take one of our small cities of equal rank in population, Oswego, N. Y., or Springfield, O., for instance, and imagine that there were in either city a small minority like that of the Gentiles in Salt Lake City, the capital of Utah, having the same privileges. In addition, to make the parallel more complete, imagine this minority non-Christian, say Jews, Infidels, and Pagans, and that they should continuously denounce their Christian fellow-citizens as knaves, as frauds, as whore-mongers, their wives as prostitutes and their children as bastards. To make the comparison still closer, we must further imagine that in this small minority there were comprised all the gamblers, all the land-sharks, all the rum-sellers, all the public prostitutes, together with all their patrons. What exhibition of Christian meekness would you look for from Oswego or Springfield Christians?

But again to the *facts?*

Every denomination of religion is guaranteed the fullest protection by Mormon law, and their Church edifices exemption from taxation. At the first annual celebration of their arrival in Utah, called the harvest feast, July 24, 1848, they sang a hymn of which the following is a portion:

Come, ye Christian sects and pagans,
 Indian, Moslem, Greek and Jew,
Worshippers of God or Dagon,
 Freedom's banner waves for you.

Brigham Young gave over one thousand dollars to the erection of non-Mormon Churches in Salt Lake City. He gave five hundred dollars for this purpose to the Catholics, liberally to the Episcopal chapel, and a plot of land to the Jews for a cemetery. When divines of reputation visit Salt Lake City they have been invariably offered the pulpit of the Tabernacle. R. N. Baskin, ex-U. S. Prosecuting Attorney, and well known as an anti-Mormon and persistent "turf-hunter," testified as follows before the House Committee on Territories, January 21, 1870:

I have been for five years a resident of Utah. I must do the Mormons the justice to say that the question of religion does not enter into their courts, in ordinary cases; I have never detected any bias on the part of jurors there in this respect, as I at first expected; I have appeared in cases where Mormons and Gentiles were opposing parties in the case, and saw, much to my surprise, the jury do what is right.

From a pamphlet issued in 1878 by A. Milton Musser, a "Mormon Elder," I make the following extract, and from my personal experience in the Territory since my first visit there, in 1879, I honestly believe that his proud boast is the absolute truth:

Out of the twenty counties in the Territory, most of which are populous, thirteen are to-day without a dram shop, brewery, gambling or brothel house, bowling or billiard saloon, *lawyer, doctor, parson, beggar, politician or place-hunter*, and almost entirely free from social troubles of every kind, yet these counties are exclusively " Mormon," and, with the exception of a now and then domestic doctor or lawyer, the entire Territory was free from these adjuncts of civilization (?) till after the advent of the professing Christian element, boastingly here to "regenerate" the " Mormons," and to-day every single disreputable concern in Utah is run and fostered by the very same Christian (?) elements. Oaths, imprecations, blasphemies, invectives, expletives, blackguardism, the ordinary dialect of the anti-" Mormon " were not heard in Utah till after his advent; nor, till then, did we have litigation, drunkenness, harlotry, political and judicial deviltries, gambling and kindred enormities.

Extortion and excessive usury are forbidden. A " Mormon " merchant would at once jeopardise his fellowship if he made a " corner " on any article found only in his store, no matter how great the demand. We never go to law except when we are forced to.

We are taught to treat the Indians with kindness and consideration, and never to take advantage of their ignorance in purchasing their land claims, robes, buckskins, or furs. We have lived among them for thirty years, with comparatively little bloodshed or trouble.

Our course has always been to feed, clothe, and teach them the arts of civilization, and to school their children. *No half-breed "Mormon" Indian children are found in all our borders.* In the constitution of the State of *Deseret*, in which name Utah hopes soon to be admitted into the union of States, the " Mormons " further exhibit their liberality by inserting a clause in favor of *minority* representation in our political assemblages, notwithstanding the number of anti-"Mormons" is not over seven per cent. of the entire population. These are but a very few of the evidences of " Mormon " generosity to non-" Mormons " and their institutions.

Do you say that this broad liberality—giving use of public halls free of rent to weak religious societies, or money to aid them to build antagonistic Churches, and careful provision for minority representation, is but crafty " policy?" Granted; but in that case bear in mind that the second generation of Mormons is now on the stage, and the third is growing up, then tell us how many generations can be brought up under this " policy " without being governed by it and permeated with its spirit. Nor need we cross the Rockies for an illustration of illiberality. In Vermont the State represented by Mr. Morrill, father of the anti-polygamy law of 1862, Mr. Poland, and Mr. Edmunds, each authors or sponsors for bills of still more sweeping nature, the overwhelming majority of the voters are Republicans, and inherit their Whig fathers' aversion to Democrats. How have they used this great preponderance in numbers ? Let me recall an instance falling within my own knowledge. In most of the smaller New England towns the use of the Town Hall is given to each political party for their meetings without charge. During our Civil War in some of these towns the Democrats were refused the use of the Town Hall upon the ground that their party was a " disloyal " organization; and even as late as the campaign of 1868, in Springfield, Vt., the same rule was rigorously enforced !

In view of the facts I have given, if we were to look for advocates of the American principles of toleration and equal justice, together with recognition of minority rights, should we look to Vermont for the supply and to Utah for their field of operations, or *vice versâ ?*

Let us now consider more closely the moral condition of the Mormons as evidenced in the criminal records. *Facts* are worth more than assertions, and there is probably no subject before the American people concerning which so much is said, in which there is such widespread ignorance of facts as in the Mormon question. It is our duty to study all sides of it in order to deal with it dispassionately.

In Salt Lake City there are about seventy-five Mormons to twenty-five non-Mormons. In Salt Lake County there are about eighty Mormons to twenty non-Mormons. In 1882 the jailor of the County prison stated that the convicts for the five preceding years were all anti-Mormons except *three.*

In Utah we have seen from the report of the United States Census that the proportion of orthodox Mormons to all others is as eighty-three to seventeen.

In the winter of 1881-82, just previous to the operation of the Edmunds law, there were in the Utah penitentiary fifty-one prisoners, only five of whom were Mormons, and two of the five were in prison for imitating Abraham in their domestic *ménage.* So that the seventeen per cent. "outsiders" had forty-six convicts, while the eighty-three per cent. Mormons had but five! The total number of Utah lockups, including the penitentiary (covering twenty counties), was fourteen; these aggregated one hundred and twenty-five inmates. Of this number not over eleven were Mormon, several of whom were incarcerated for minor offences and polygamy.

The arrests made in Salt Lake City during 1881 are classified as follows:

Men	782
Women	200
Boys	38
Total	1,020

Mormon—Men and Boys	163	
" Women	6	169
Non-Mormon—Men and Boys	657	
" " Women	194	851
		1,020

A number of the Mormon arrests were for petty offences and water trespass. The arrests of the non-Mormons were largely for drunkenness, prostitution, gambling, exposure of person, unlawful dram-selling, assault and battery, attempt to kill, etc.

If the seventy-five per cent. Mormon population of Salt Lake City had been as lawless and corrupt as the record shows the twenty-five per cent. non-Mormons to have been, there would have been 2,443 arrests from their ranks during the year 1881, instead of the comparatively trifling number of 169 shown on the record; while if the twenty-five per cent. non-Mormon population (embracing the full membership of the various churches in that city) had been as law-abiding and upright as the seventy-five per cent. Mormon population, instead of the startling number of 851 arrests, they would have furnished but 56 ! Thus with three quarters of the population, the Mormons furnished less than one-sixth of the arrests.

The criminal statistics of Utah are kept with more than customary precision and care, and furnish an accurate record of the belief as well as the crime of the prisoner. The statistics for 1882, the first year of the *moral* crusade inaugurated by the fervid zeal of our own St. Jerome, furnish equally interesting data. Taking in all the popu· lous districts of the Territory, the total number of arrests for crimes and misdemeanors in these localities during the year 1882, was two thousand one hundred and ninety-eight, of which the Mormon population furnished three hundred, and the non-Mormon minority one thousand eight hundred and ninety-eight.

Taking the whole number of arrests reported in the Territory, we find the vastly preponderating number of Mormons contributing but one-eighth of the cases recorded, and the non-Mormons seven-eighths !

A writer in the *Chicago Times* from Salt Lake City, under date of January 24, 1884, commenting on the above, remarks:

The number of brothels throughout the Territory was twelve, all kept by non-Mormons; number of inmates not given.

The criminal record of Salt Lake City, for 1882, shows that in a population of about twenty-five thousand, divided between Mormons and non-Mormons as nineteen to six, the total number of arrests was one thousand five hundred and sixty-one, of which one hundred and eighty-eight were Mormons, and one thousand three hundred and seventy-three non-Mormons. Classed by sex, the number of Mormon men and boys was one hundred and seventy-seven; non-Mormon, one thousand two hundred and seventy-one: Mormon women, eleven; non-Mormon, one hundred and three. Of the sixty-six houses where beer and liquor were retailed by the glass, sixty were kept by non-Mormons, and the remaining six, nominally Mormons, were not entitled to participate in the sacraments of the Church by reason of their calling. The fifteen billiard rooms and bowling alleys and the seven gambling houses were all kept by non-Mormons. The six brothels had non-Mormon proprietors, and they were filled by thirty-one non-Mormon inmates.

If it should be suspected that these territorial and city exhibits show an unfair discrimination in favor of the Mormon population, through the sympathy of the Mormon police officers and magistrates such suspicion will be removed by the summary of the records of the territorial penitentiary for the same year. It will be recollected that for the conviction of this class of criminals, the whole machinery of the law, judicial and ministerial, is in the hands of the Federal government. The number of penitentiary convicts for the year was twenty-eight. Of these but one was an orthodox Mormon, and she a woman, confined for one day for contempt of court; five others were Mormons only by reason of their parentage, and the remaining twenty-two were eight Catholics, four Methodists, one Jew, one Adventist, one Presbyterian, and seven of no religious faith.

The tabular statement of the arrests throughout the Territory for 1882 furnishes food for varied reflection. One application only will be made. If those practicing polygamy are, as a class, actuated by the licentious motives with which they are charged, why is it that the affiliated crimes of prostitution, brothel-keeping, lewd conduct, insulting women, exposing person, attempting rape, and obscene and profane language, occasioning in all one hundred and seventy-nine arrests, are so nearly monopolized by the non-Mormon element that the proportion should be thirty-five to one? Crime breeds its congeners; and does not this table of crime furnish proof of the general honesty of those who enter the polygamic state?

While perhaps sufficient evidence has been produced to show how little danger there is of *our morals* becoming perverted by association with the distant Mormons, still, to make the record complete I cite the criminal statistics, hitherto unpublished in detail, for the year 1885. Taken in connection with the above extract on a detailed statement of crimes for the year 1882, it will furnish suggestive reflections. These figures are official, having been taken from the city records. They are as follows:

CRIMINAL STATISTICS OF SALT LAKE CITY FOR THE YEAR 1885.

Estimated population of the City 26,000, one fifth of whom are estimated to be non-Mormons, or Gentiles as they are called.

	Mormons.	Non Mormons.
Assault with deadly weapons with intent to kill		
Assault and Battery...................	8	112
" Provoking...................		
Assaulting Officers...................		
Burglary...............................	0	19
Counterfeiting.........................	0	4
Contempt of Court.....................	0	2
Concealing stolen property.............	0	1
Drunk and disorderly.................		
" " profane.................		
" " trespass	41	474
" " vagrancy		
Destroying property....................	1	12
Disturbing the peace...................	10	65
Discharging fire-arms..................	2	2
Doing business without license..........	2	15
Desertion from U. S. Army..............	0	3
Exposing person.......................	0	3
Embezzlement	0	5

	Mormons.	Non-Mormons.
Forgery	0	4
Fighting	5	27
Gambling and keeping gambling houses ...	0	44
Highway robbery......................	0	4
House-breaking	0	3
Ill-fame house keeping	0	12
Inmates of "	0	41
Insulting ladies......................	0	6
Opium house keeping..................	0	3
Disorderly house......................	0	1
Lewd conduct.........................	0	16
Larceny, grand and petit...............	7	79
Murder...............................	0	1
Obtaining goods under false pretences	0	9
Prostitution	0	3
Profanity and obscenity................	3	20
Rape, intent to commit................	0	2
Resisting officers.....................	3	4
Stealing railroad rides.................	0	22
Selling liquor without license to Indians, on Sunday, etc.,......................	0	3
Threatening violence, and to kill..........	0	12
Trespass..............................	1	39
Vagrancy	0	51
Miscellaneous, or minor, offences........	13	49
Total No. arrests..................	96	1,180
		96
Grand Total No....................		1,276
Adults Males....................	1,136	
" Females.................	134	
Boys under 10 years old..........	16	1,276
Total estimated population...........		26,000
Mormons..........................	20,800	
Non-Mormons	5,200	26,000

or 5 Mormons to 1 non-Mormon.

The 20,800 Mormons produce arrests...		96
The 5,200 non-Mormons " " ...		1,180

or 1 to 12⅓ !

Most all the vilest, vicious and infamous crimes were committed by the non-Mormons. Among the arrests for *lewd and lascivious cohabitation* were U. S. Deputy Marshal Oscar Vandercook; Ass't. U. S. Deputy Jos. Bush; Ass't. U. S. Deputy Prosecuting Attorney S. H. Lewis; Ex-U. S. Commissioner Charles Pearson, and other prominent anti-Mormons. Many of the complaints lodged at Police

Headquarters against the Gentiles arrested were made by Gentiles. Every other town, city and county, being less affected and influenced by outside influence, and all the jails and the Utah penitentiary, show a much cleaner record in favor of the Mormons, compared with the anti-Mormon record, than the foregoing record of the capital city portrays.

The following are the numbers of arrests made by the city police during the first four months of the current year, viz: 1886:

	Mormons.	Non-Mormons.
January	9	34
February	4	54
March	4	74
April	6	87
Totals	23	249
Mormons		23
Non-Mormons		249
Grand Total		272

1 Mormon to 11 non-Mormons for the four months.

That Mormon judges are impartial and fair in dealing with all classes of criminals, is fully attested by the following certificates from a rabid anti-Mormon source:

No more just or better man sat on the bench of the police court of this city than Justice Spiers. * * * Justice Spiers is one of the best, if not the best, man on the whole People's ticket.

Salt Lake Daily Tribune, Feb. 8, 1884.

At another time the same paper referred to the late alderman Pyper in even stronger terms of commendation than the foregoing. For years past Aldermen Pyper and Spiers have been the principal justices under whom the municipal prosecutions have been conducted in Salt Lake City.

We need not be surprised, then, in view of the appalling criminal record above disclosed of the non-Mormon population, that a Mormon friend, in writing to me, should make use of the following expressions:

If the local enemies of Utah had such a showing to offer, they would never cease referring to their comparatively clean record. The pulpit and press would bull the refrain from river to ocean, and Talmadge, Cook, *et al.*, the anti-Mormon rabbis of clean Brooklyn and cleaner Boston, would go fairly wild over the discovery. Day and night the local cabal would laud and extol themselves and theirs

as the veritable Saints juxtaposed by the side of the Mormons, and if
the Mormons would not purge themselves of their uncleanness, they
would be driven into Salt Lake *nolens volens.*

President Taylor and Geo. Q. Cannon, in their "Epistle of the
First Presidency" to the Annual Conference at Provo City, April
6th, 1886, make use of the following language, which can be contested by no one familiar with this subject-matter:

There are now in this city some six brothels, forty tap-rooms,
a number of gambling houses, pool tables and other disreputable
concerns, *all* run by non-Mormons.   But for the presence of those
who are constantly making war upon us, our city would be free from
the contaminating influences of houses of prostitution, gambling
houses, dram shops and other such death-dealing concerns, and the
taxes would be greatly reduced.   But, as it is, the Mormons are
forced to pay a liberal tax in support of the laws against the lawless-
ness of their non tax-paying enemies.   Every other town, city and
county in the Territory, and all the jails and the Utah penitentiary,
show even a much cleaner record in favor of the "Mormons" than
the foregoing exhibit portrays.
If it should be said that these convictions were made by
"Mormon" judges and justices, it must also be remembered that
the District Court always stands open and gladly extends relief to
any who consider themselves wronged by "Mormon" officers.

We have seen that the Mormons are a prosperous, well-to-do
people, believing in co-operation, and averse to litigation as a means
of settling disputes.   The *à priori* conclusion that such a people
would naturally incline to moral paths and rectitude of character,
we have seen signally borne out by the facts.   Can such a people
be steeped in gross ignorance?   Again we must appeal to the *facts.*

We hear among other methods advised for "wiping out" Mormonism, some of the effects of which we have been considering, that
of education.   In presenting some statistical information upon this
subject, let us bear in mind the peculiar circumstances under which
Utah is placed.   Her population is not recruited from the schools
and colleges of free lands; their growth, like that of another Church
in the first century, is not the result of drawing-room *soirées* or social
patronage.   The Mormon population came largely from countries
where the peasantry are not the most cultured and enlightened; persons who never studied in the Oscar Wilde school of esthetics, or
danced attendance at the doors of a green-room to catch a smile
from Lily Langtry; and who, either from past poverty or present
isolation have not had the advantages enjoyed by us.
A recent article in *Harper's Magazine* cavalierly described the

bulk of the Mormon "peasantry" as "low, base-born foreigners," thereby implying as a reproach the semi-serfdom in which they had been so long enthralled in the Christian countries which they gladly left for a home of their own in the West. Before citing the census reports of 1880, let us take that of 1870 and compare Utah with some of the more favored States, when Utah was even more decidedly Mormon than to-day.

COMPARATIVE STATISTICS.	School attendance, 5 to 18 years.	Illiteracy; can't read or write, 10 years and upward.	Paupers.	Insane and Idiotic.	Convicts.	Printing and Publishing Establishmt's	Church Attendance.
Utah............................	35	11	6	5	3	14	19
United States...............	31	26	31	16	9	6	17
Pennsylvania	30	10	45	17	9	9	14
New York....................	21	9	59	20	12	7	12
Massachusetts	25	12	55	23	11	11	12
Dist. of Columbia...........	27	40	23	35	9	11	8
California....................	24	10	41	22	19	14	9

A Church emigration agency was established in Liverpool as long ago as 1840, and since that time upwards of 80,000 persons have availed themselves of the advantageous rates secured thereby to emigrants from Europe. A very large proportion of these have been assisted either by the P. E. Fund, established for that purpose, or by means which relatives in this country have forwarded to them. They are most generally from the northern portions of Europe, from those hardy races in which freedom first arose and has been most stubbornly defended. A shipping agent for a line of steamers from Liverpool says: "The class of persons in the Mormon emigration are generally intelligent and well behaved, and many of them are highly respectable. The means taken by this people for the preservation of order and cleanliness on board are admirable, and worthy of imitation. It is a general complaint with captains that the quantity of luggage put on board with Mormons quite takes them by surprise, and often sinks the ship upwards of an inch deeper in the water than they would otherwise allow her to go."

The amount invested in school property was returned as being about eighteen and one half dollars per capita of the school population. In contrast with this take the amount per capita of their school population which some of the States have invested in school property: North Carolina, less than 60 cents; Louisiana, $3.00; Virginia about $2.00; Oregon less than $9.00; Wisconsin less than

$11.00; Tennessee, less than $2.50; Delaware, less than $13.00. In respect to the amount per capita of its school population which Utah has invested in school property, it exceeds that of several other Southern and Western States, is in advance of the great States of Indiana and Illinois, and in excess of the general average of the entire Union.

In the matter of education, Utah stands ahead of many old and wealthy States, and of the general average of the United States in three very important respects, namely, the enrollment of her school population, the percentage of their daily attendance at school and the amount per capita invested in school property. When it is remembered that in nearly every State in the Union, vast sums of money derived from the sale of lands or from the establishment of special funds are devoted to school purposes, and that these sums amount to tens or hundreds of thousands of dollars annually, in many of the States, while the schools of Utah have never yet received any assistance whatever in this manner, the fact that the Territory occupies its present advanced position in respect to education, speaks highly in praise of its legislators. A Territorial tax equal to that from which the entire revenue of that country is derived is annually assessed, collected, and disbursed exclusively for payment of school teachers in district schools, open to the children of all citizens, irrespective of creed or color, no religious tenets being incorporated in their text books. Further, a local option law permits a tax not exceeding two per cent. for general school purposes to be annually assessed in the district where the people so elect by popular vote.

The school age is from six to eighteen, and the school population in 1881 was 42,353, with an average daily attendance of 44 per cent. The number of schools in 1879 was 373; in 1880, 374; in 1881, 395; and in 1883, 411.

In the average amount paid monthly per teacher for services, Utah stands ahead of not only the general average, but of many States and some of the Territories. The general average is $36.21; Utah, $42.48; the lowest being $21.27. And in this connection the census shows that the State which produced Utah's most inveterate enemies, Vermont, regards the value of school teachers to a community at the low figure of $21.81 per month.

A special committee of the Nevada State Senate several years since in a report, praised the school system of Utah as "unsurpassed in its adaptation to the wants of the masses." The Constitution adopted by the people when seeking admission into the Union as a State, and framed entirely by Mormon delegates, contains the following:

"ARTICLE XI.

"*Section* 1.—The legislature shall provide for a uniform system of public schools, and may establish free schools, *provided* that no sectarian or denominational doctrines shall be taught in any school supported in whole or in part by public funds.

"*Sec.* 2.—All legislation in regard to education shall be impartial, guaranteeing to all persons, of every race, color and religion, equal rights and privileges.

"*Sec.* 3.—No religious sect or denomination shall ever control or appropriate to its own use any of the public school or university funds of the State."

Henry Randall Waite, Statistician of the Tenth United States Census, has publicly made the following charge against the people of Utah; "We find a system of public schools established under laws whose provisions are capable of being so construed as to debar non-Mormons from becoming teachers, and which in violation of a fundamental principle of our government are used for the propagation of religious tenets."

In reply to this statement it will be sufficient to cite the following official list of

Text books in use in the District Schools.

Independent Series of Readers.
Watson's Complete Speller.
Ray's New Elementary Arithmetic.
Ray's New Practical Arithmetic.
Appleton's Standard Elementary Geography.
Appleton's Standard Higher Geography.
Swinton's New Language Lessons.
Spencerian System of Copy Books, Writing and Penmanship.
Anderson's Popular History of the United States.
Krusi's System of Drawing.

From the report of the Chancellor of the University of Deseret, which institution has about 300 students, I make the following extract:

"The University has now within itself many elements of prosperity; it only needs the sustaining power of the Legislature to make it adequate to meet the increasing educational requirements of our prosperous Territory. It is, so far as an institution within its scope of patronage can be made, a practical institution; *it is also non-sectarian* in its character and conducted in such a manner as to *avoid giving a bias* in the pupils' minds in favor of any particular form of religion. The fact that it has been non-sectarian has been, in the minds of some of our citizens, an objection to the institution. The charge has been made that the tendency of its teaching has been to favor infidelity in religion and doubts respecting the existence of God. The University has had this prejudice to contend with, and on this account many have felt some reluctance about permitting their children to become its pupils. Such persons have not clearly understood that the character of the institution did not permit religious instruction, and because religious teaching was not imparted in its classes, the conclusion has been jumped at that its influence must necessarily be in the direction of infidelity. I scarcely need say that this feeling has no basis of truth for its support. While avoiding all sectarian teaching the Chancellor and Board of Regents have been careful to impress upon the President of the institution the importance of not permitting any books to reach the pupils or any teaching to be imparted to them that would have the effect, in the slightest degree, to weaken their belief in and reverence for the Supreme Being or the cardinal truths of Christianity universally accepted throughout Christendom. They have felt that while it was not proper, under the circumstances, for religious instruction to be given within the institution, neither was its province to teach infidelity. The true character of the institution is now better known, and parents in sending their children to be taught have done so with the understanding that they are to be instructed only in those branches which belong to a school of this character. The studies are so conducted that the children of parents, of all sects or of no sect, can share in them with the utmost propriety and freedom.

A few extracts taken from the census of the United States for 1880, pertaining to Utah, showing a comparison of illiteracy, etc., with several states of the Union, and the United States, may be of interest.

Of the population of Utah one quarter are under eight years old, one third under eleven, and one half under seventeen. Utah has more children under five years old, in proportion to its population, than any other division of the country, but Arkansas is very nearly abreast of her, for Utah has 1776 children under five years old in every 10,000 of the population, while Arkansas has 1775 in the same number. When we reach ten years Utah loses her supremacy. At this point the number in each 1000 souls is—Arkansas, 337; Mississippi, 333; Texas, 331; Alabama, 325; Utah, 324; Georgia, 319; the whole of the United States, 267. Per contra we will take some of the United States where the proportion is below the average—New York, 216; Vermont, 205; Massachusetts, 205; Colorado, 185.

NUMBER OF ADULTS, MINORS, AND MINORS OF LEGAL SCHOOL AGE, IN EACH 100 INHABITANTS, 1880:

	Adults.	Minors.	Minors of legal school age.
Montana....................	69	31	24
Nevada.....................	67	33	16
Vermont....................	58	42	30
New York...................	57	43	33
Maryland and Ohio...........	51	49	34
New Mexico.................	51	49	24
United States...............	50	50	32
Virginia	46	54	39
Tennessee	44	56	37
Utah	43	57	30
South Carolina..............	43	57	26

There were in 1880 in:

	Schools.	School buildings.	Valued at
Utah	383	334	$372,273
Nevada	185	93	282,870
New Mexico........	162	46	13,500
Arizona............	101	84	113,074
Idaho	127	112	31,000
Wyoming	55	29	40,500

Races in school population, of legal school age:

Utah.	Males.	Females.
Native	16,659	18,937
Foreign	2,312	2,324
Colored ....:.	148	134
	22,119	21,395

And in this connection I would correct an erroneous impression that the great bulk of the Mormons are foreign born. In Utah and the adjacent States and Territories it is probable that the Mormons number nearly 250,000. We have seen that the total immigration for forty years past, has amounted to about 80,000, living and dead.

According to the U. S. Census of 1880, the following States and Territories have a larger proportion of foreign-born population than Utah:

	Native Born.	Foreign Born.
California	571,820	292,874
Arizona	24,391	16,040
Dakota	83,382	51,795
Minnesota	513,697	267,676
Nevada	36,615	25,653
Wisconsin	910,072	415,425
UTAH	99,969	43,994

Some other States and Territories have nearly as large a percentage of foreign born. Even New York having 1,211,389 foreign born as against 3,871,492 native born.

STATISTICS OF ILLITERACY, AS GIVEN IN THE CENSUS OF 1880.

	PerCent UTAH.	PerCent RHODE ISLAND.	PerCent UNITED STATES.
Persons of 10 years and upward, who cannot read.........	5.0	7.9	13.4
" " " " " write	9.1	11.2	17.0
Whites " " " " "	8.5	10.9	9.4
Native whites, of 10 years and upward, who cannot write...	5.9	2.9	8.7
Foreign " " " " " " ...	11.8	27.3	12.0
Whites, 10 to 14 inclusive, who cannot write.............	10.7	8.3	11.9
" " " " " Males........	11.9	9.0	13.0
" " " " " Females......	9.5	7.6	10.7
" 15 to 20 " " "	4.9	9.1	7.2
" " " " " Males........	5.8	9.5	7.8
" " " " " Females......	3.9	8.6	6.7
" 21 and upward, who cannot write...............	8.9	11.7	9.4

I have taken Rhode Island because it is a typical manufacturing. State, and, like Utah, has a large foreign-born population. Of the forty-seven States and Territories enumerated in the Census returns, twenty-six (including Massachusetts) exhibit a higher percentage of total population over ten years of age unable to read, and twenty unable to write. The State having the highest percentage is Alabama, where Mormons have been mobbed. That State shows a percentage of 43.5 unable to read, and of 50.9 unable to write, or over half the population in a State where the colored people are in a minority of over 60,000.

Thus we find the average illiteracy in Utah, among persons of all ages, is less than the average of the country, as a whole; and leaving out both the colored and foreign-born population, and taking only the native whites of ten years of age and upwards, Utah's percentage of illiteracy is exceeded in twenty States and Territories, Indiana being one of the number. The percentage of lunatics, paupers and criminals is also much lower than the general average.

In view of these *facts*, is it not well for us to pause before we join in the wholesale denunciation made by Christian ministers concerning the ignorance prevailing where a "priesthood" is alleged to dominate? In thrift and enterprise; in social well being; in social checks to the development of greed; in the cultivation of amity and the elimination of the monopolist on the one hand and the strife-breeding lawyer on the other; in the peaceful possession of unmortgaged homes; in general morality and care taken to extend the

blessings of education, where is there a Christian community in all
our broad land that can hurl the first stone at the sober, industrious
and peace-loving Mormon. A calm investigation of *facts* is alone
sufficient to show that the animus of the crusade on the Mormons is
plunder. The following are the kinds and percentage of taxes im-
posed by law on the people of Utah, and the taxes of no other Territory or State can make as favorable an exhibit:

Territorial tax.	. . . .	3 mills on the dollar.
County "	. . . .	6 " " "
City "	. . .	5 " " "
School "	. .	3 " " "

Only 17 mills on the dollar including City tax. Outside of city
limits the tax is but 12 mills on the dollar. Every unprejudiced
person in Utah knows that if the anti-Mormons were in control of
the Territory, as they are scheming in Congress to be, that the
Territory, and every county and city, would soon be overwhelmed
with debt, and taxation under carpet-bag rule would soon become
decupled.

We have seen the cause of the opposition of the commercial
monopolist and of the legal fraternity; we now see why they have
enlisted with them the political gamesters and governmental prostitutes, who scent in the air not only prospective offices, but plunder
of as mean and despicable a character as ever disgraced a Roman
consul in the later days of the Roman Republic. Adroitly fanning
the spark of religious bigotry in the breast of the straight-laced
Evangelical proselyter, ever ready to burst into flame, our Protestant
pulpits throughout the land offer their prayers and " pass the plate "
to hasten the day when Christian civilization shall break down the
wall of social co-operation against which it is surging, when the prose-
lyting dominie and the bedizened harlot, the rumseller and the pettifogger, the gambler and the long-faced hypocrite, may enter arm in
arm to divide the spoils. Is it worth our while to break down this
system for the inimitable privilege of extending Christian churches
and hellish brothels; of erecting by the side of the school-house a
gin mill with a faro-table accompaniment; of introducing the extor-
tioner and usurer to fatten on the industry of unburdened farmers,
and increase the business of the sheriffs at their expense; to convert
peaceful hamlets into mining camps, and offer a premium for the
importation of broken-down political adventurers rejected at home?
The whole crusade is but a huge adventurer's raffle, in which prizes
can only be won by ruthlessly trampling upon all moral decency and

natural right, in which the sleek hypocrite and the unblushing harlot jostle each other in their avaricious race for spoils, and push the soulless adventurers on with prayers and favors.

This crusade upon the peaceful and law-abiding inhabitants of Utah is only paralleled in modern history by the "No-Popery" madness of our English ancestors, when crowds went wild with joy when a Catholic was sent to the scaffold; when test oaths were framed by jurists to fan the flame of religious bigotry, ostensibly in the interest of the State, but really for the personal aggrandizement of political prostitutes whose sole idea of heaven was the enjoyment of office and perquisites; when human vermin like Titus Oates, reeking with slander and falsehood, were honored and revered; when judges in the interest of the abstraction—the general will—trampled upon and derided every individual right and grew rich from harvesting where they had not sown. Judges, like Sir Thomas More, have sat on the bench and condemned poor old women to the stake for the imaginary crime of witchcraft to defend an equally imaginary *social* morality. Again, judges, like the infamous Jeffries, in the name of law and with the support of a hireling judiciary, have sent school-girls to prison and innocent men and women to the gallows, "general repute" being sufficient evidence in the eyes of bigoted or professional jurors.

America, like England, has her Tories. The fiction of "divine right to govern" is still loudly asserted by modern Jeffries, relying on modern Titus Oates and professional jurors, though the somewhat threadbare mantle of grace has been stretched to cover with its folds the hungry and ambitious pettifoggers we permit to misrepresent us in the halls of Congress. The same persecuting spirit that overflowed the narrow soul of the religious bigot in the interest of a Protestant State, to-day is rampant in equally contracted souls in the interest of the Commercial State. The penny-pinching trader, the strife-begetting pettifogger, the political prostitute and spoils gambler, flanked by various grades of Salvation Army exhorters and shameless harlots, with shrill and discordant voices cry out in the name of law to stifle liberty because, like their illustrious prototype Demetrius, the silversmith of Ephesus, "this our craft is in danger to be set at nought!"

CHAPTER V.

PLURAL MARRIAGE.

BEFORE entering upon a discussion of the methods adopted by the Government in Utah to suppress unlawful cohabitation, under what is known as the Edmunds act, it will be well to first obtain a somewhat clear and definite idea of what polygamy is in its American, or Mormon, form, and the reasons why a whole people cling to it with such tenacity. I have stated that I did not regard polygamy as the real issue, and have given reasons to show that the governing motive was at bottom an economic one, a desire to break down a social system founded upon co-operation and arbitration. In such a work it is not strange that facts should be distorted and gross misrepresentations should abound. It is not my purpose to enter upon the legal aspect of polygamy, or the abstract right or wrong of the institution, but merely whether it is such "an overt act against peace and good order," as to warrant the general crusade inaugurated. All we have here to consider is if Mormon plural marriage can be so designated.

The Colonial Congress which met in September, 1774, set forth their grievances in language so appropriate to the present state of affairs in Utah, that I must call the attention of the reader to their statements:

Resolved: I. That they are entitled to life, liberty and property, and have never ceded to any sovereign power whatever a right to dispose of either without consent.

II. That our ancestors were at the time of their emigration from the mother country entitled to all the rights, liberties and immunities of free and natural-born subjects within the realm of England.

III. That by such emigration they have neither forfeited, surrendered nor lost any of those rights.

IV. That the foundation of English liberty, and of all free government, is a right of the people to participate in their legislative councils.

V. That, therefore, the exercise of legislative power in several colonies, by a council appointed during the pleasure of the crown, is unconstitutional, dangerous, and destructive to the freedom of American legislation.

Our forefathers in adopting these resolutions were not deterred by the Tory charge that they were assailing "the sacredness of law," but firmly placed themselves on natural rights, and became rebels to sustain them. Here the parallel ends, for the citizens of Utah have not, nor do they propose to, array themselves by overt acts against even unjust and tyrannical laws.

Let us also bear in mind that the practice has the sanction of the Old Testament and is nowhere condemned in the New; and that when entered into upon religious grounds the question under our laws is whether the relation in itself is such as to warrant extreme measures for the protection of society. This can only be determined by again appealing to the *facts*.

Taking the census of six years ago as basis for numerical state-ments, Utah had far more than double the population of Nevada, a State, and more than that of Kansas and Nebraska combined when they were admitted into the Union. How many women are there in what popular imagination pictures as a vast harem? In 1880 Massachusetts had a surplus of females of over 64,000. Over 64,000 condemned to be old maids and fail to fulfil the law of their being, or to fill the ranks of prostitutes crowding the streets of our cities. The census returns show twenty-two States having a surplus of females, while in Utah there are and always have been more males than females. The number of Mormons living in plural marriage does not exceed two per cent. of the entire male population. Emi-grants are invariably sought in families, and if the statistics of Castle Garden are obtainable it will be seen that there is no differ-ence in this respect between Mormon immigrants and others.

Is it then true that this minority of polygamists constitute an aristocracy, a new "slaveocracy," holding free expression of opinion in abeyance? So far from this being true, we have seen the liberality of their legislation. Further, the Mormons have established woman suffrage, and as the new Edmunds bill now before Congress abolishes this right, ostensibly in the interest of women, I will cite certain sections from the Utah election laws.

In section 1 the following form of oath or affirmation is given:

TERRITORY OF UTAH, ⎰
COUNTY ———, ⎱ *ss.*

I, ——— ———, being first duly sworn, depose and say that I am over twenty-one years of age and have resided in the Territory of Utah for six months and in the precinct of ——— one month next preceding the date hereof, and (if a male) am a ("native born," or "naturalized," as the case may be) citizen of the United States, and a tax payer in this Territory; (or, if a female), I am "native born," or "naturalized," or the "wife," "widow," or "daughter" (as the case may be) of a native born or naturalized citizen of the United States.

Subscribed and sworn to before me this —— day of ——, A.D., 18—.

——— ———, Assessor.

Section 13 provides that the voter shall, "on the name of the proposed voter being found on the registry list, and on all challenges being decided in favor of such voter," present his or her ballot to the proper official who shall deposit it in the ballot box, but that if "any mark whatever" be found thereon, it shall be rejected, thus impartially preserving and protecting the secrecy of the ballot. The statement that a female who is a minor and an alien can vote under the laws of Utah, or that any mark or indorsement on a ballot is permissible, is utterly baseless and untrue.

The Utah Legislature, in their Memorial to Congress in 1882, state:

When accused of exercising undue influence over the female portion of the population, and the idea was advanced that if the women in Utah were granted the right to vote, a remedy would at once be found, the Territorial Legislature promptly anticipated the proposed action of Congress, and passed an act conferring upon women in Utah, over twenty-one years of age, and with other proper qualifications, the elective franchise.

Again, when accused of making the Church dominate the State, by permitting ecclesiastical influence or priestly authority to assert influence at the polls by means of the marked ballot—which had been approved, and which many still believe to be the cheapest and best means of preventing illegal votes—the Legislature enacted a law providing for the registration of voters, repealing all election laws requiring numbered or otherwise marked ballots, and making them *strictly secret*.

So far is it from being true that undue influences exist at Utah elections, their law is far more liberal than that of many States. And the denial of all civil rights to polygamists can have no other effect than the disqualification of the prosperous well-to-do class, who in having the heaviest investments at stake are certainly conservative.

One feature of this perplexing question that should always be borne in mind is that it has its most ardent supporters among women. I assert that the most intellectual, the most moral, the most untrammeled of Mormon ladies indorse the system. And I assert this, knowing that Utah is the peer of any State in noble-minded women; women of culture and refinement constantly engaged in active work through the press, the Relief Societies, the Mutual Improvement Societies, and other agencies of benevolent action which abound wherever a Mormon settlement is found.

Here is a Territory having more males than females, yet public opinion, enlightened and religious, freely accepting polygamy as not only a divine institution, but carrying with it its own justification. The Mormon holds that God never gives a revelation without some specific end, and they believe that in polygamy lies the cure for social evils, which have made our civilization a stench in the nostrils of every moralist. Many of these ladies—some living in affluence and ease, tender mothers and loving wives, writing for and editing periodicals and shining in social circles with unaffected grace, with full liberty to follow the dictates of their own hearts—make no appeal for aid, no cry for redress, save from the tyrannical action of oppressive laws.

All over this broad land are thousands of wives broken in health and suffering from chronic diseases having their rise in sexual complications, yet who stand aloof in holy horror from a social system in which the wife and mother has more absolute control over her own person than under any system heretofore existing. The Mormon wife is taught that during the formation and growth of the embryo child, to use the words of a Mormon woman, "her heart should be pure, her thoughts and affections chaste, her mind calm, her passions without excitement, while her body should be invigorated with every exercise conducive to health and vigor, but by no means subjected to anything calculated to disturb, irritate, weary, or exhaust any of its functions. * * * Polygamy, then, as practised under the patriarchal law of God, tends directly to the chastity of women, and to sound health and morals in the constitution of their offspring."

Nor does abstinence rest here but extends over the whole period of gestation and lactation, thus comprising about two years. Remember that this is a religious belief; and I have the assurance from a lady physician of high social standing and extensive practice in Utah—a graduate of one of the best colleges in the East, and who passed several years in the hospitals of England and France—that the women of Utah are singularly free from the chronic complaints with which so many of their Eastern sisters are affected, and that their children will bear comparison with those of any other country on earth. Therefore, these healthful women smile at the epithets "misguided" and "degraded" heaped upon their heads by less healthful and less free married sisters.

Dr. Romania B. Pratt, at the Mass Meeting of Mormon women

which filled the Salt Lake Theatre on March 6, 1886, used the following language:

Our faith and confidence in the chastity and pure motives of our husbands, fathers, mothers and sons are such that we challenge the production of a better system of marriage and the records of more moral or purer lives. Hand in hand with celestial marriage is the elevation of women. In church she votes equally with men. Rights of property are given her so that she, as a married woman, can hold property in her own individual right. Women are not thrown off in old age as has been most untruthfully and shamelessly asserted. There is nothing in our plural marriage system that countenances any such thing. The very nature of the covenant forbids it. It is binding through all time and lasts throughout eternity. If any woman at an advanced period of her life wishes in a measure to retire from her husband's society with his consent, this is her own individual privilege with which no one has the right to interfere. Instances of wrong-doing may be found in families of plural households, but the exceptions are not the rule; the weight of good results of the *majority* should be the standard of judgment. It cannot be true, as asserted, that plural marriage is entered into as a rule from sensual motives. It is self-evident that it is not the case with women, and it is unreasonable to suppose that men would bring upon themselves the responsibilities, cares and expenses of a plural family, when they could avoid all this, yet revel in sin, and, in the language of a distinguished man of the world, "be like the rest of us."

We must bear in mind three fundamental facts in considering plural marriage as existing among the Latter-Day Saints:

1. The marriage is not merely for time, "till death do you part," but is a solemn covenant entered into, believed to last throughout eternity.

2. A plural marriage cannot be contracted without the consent of the first and other wives, if more than one; further that the obligation of chastity in all Mormon communities is held to be as rigorously obligatory upon the man as upon the woman, society visiting its infraction by a man there, as we would that by a woman here.

3. The responsibility is heaviest upon the man, he having no avenue of escape, while the plural wife may obtain a separation if she finds further union undesirable and unbearable.

Let us ever bear in mind that the question for us is not whether the better system prevails in Utah, but whether holding such views and refusing to disavow solemn covenants entered into by mutual consent of all parties concerned, is a just and sufficient reason to outlaw men and women from all civil rights?

Elder A. M. Musser, in describing polygamy, says:

The prevailing idea that its practice encourages excess and license, is a great mistake; the opposite to this obtains. The re-

straints of our religion are rigid and inexorable. In the rare examples of infidelity that arise in our midst, as a rule, we load most of
the responsibility on the man and make him assume most of the
odium which attaches to the sin. The helpless woman is not tabooed
and cast off with her innocent child, homeless and friendless, to
wander of necessity into deeper infamy and shame, and the man
turned loose to make other victims; he is made to take her, provide
for her, live with and respect her as he agreed to before her humilia-
tion.

The Mormons have no poor in Utah, going about unfed, un-
clothed, unschooled, or unhoused. Until the *anti-*" Mormons " came
among us we had no organ-grinders, monkey-showmen, houses of
prostitution, dram-shops, bowling saloons, and indeed but very little
of the general make-up of civilized (?) communities.

Our wives, about whose duress so much is said, enjoy greater
freedom and more franchises than any other women of the United
States. They vote on all political, social, religious, domestic, and
other general questions,—and they vote just as they please, without
let or hindrance, just as men do. [Further, they have the privilege
of nominating their husbands, and if their husbands maltreat, neglect,
or in any manner abuse them, *on their own individual application*,
without feeing a lawyer, or other expense, they can obtain a separation from them, retaining the minor children, with ample dower for
their mutual support, while their husbands *cannot divorce* their wives
except for the violation of the seventh commandment.] No woman
in Utah is barred—except by nature—the honorable and enviable
privilege of becoming a beloved wife and doting mother, which Gail
Hamilton says " is the sole, complete elysium of woman, and there is
not one woman in a million who would not be married if she had a
chance."

We maintain that women have just as much right to enjoy the
blessings of marriage and maternity, as man has to become an
honored husband and father; and as long as there is one redundant
marriageable woman in all the land, it is ungenerous, ignoble, and
cruel in man, by the proscriptive laws he ordains and enforces, to
deny her the inestimable privilege. With us marriages are consum-
mated *for* eternity, as well as time. There is no marrying in the
resurrection; it must be attended to here, the same as baptism, etc.
Godly marriage, plural or single, means healthy, beautiful offspring,
and never-ending companionship. Our system is scriptural, natural
and logical. It effectually bars the social evil, promotes longevity,
gives *every* woman a husband and a home, and multiplies the
" noblest work of God " by filling the earth with joyous, robust children.

President Geo. Q. Cannon has stated the Mormon view on this
point very clearly, and as it may be regarded as official, I will cite
his words. He says:

There is an impression among the uninformed that the man
who enters into patriarchal marriage in Utah has but little, if any,

responsibility connected with it; that upon his partners rest all the burdens and unpleasant features of the relationship; that they, in becoming his wives, become the creatures of his will, and that, therefore, their civil rights are interfered with. This view is wholly incorrect. It is the women, under the system of patriarchal marriage, who have liberty, and not the men. When once marriage has taken place between the parties, be the woman ever so poor and friendless, ever so much an unprotected stranger in the land, the man who knows her takes upon himself a life-long obligation to care for her and the fruit of their union. For a man to seek for a divorce is almost unheard of, the liberty upon this point rests with the woman; and as regards a separation, if her position should become irksome or distasteful to her, even, and she should desire a separation, not only is the man bound to respect the expressal of her wish to that effect, but he is bound also to give her and her offspring a proportionate share of his whole property. They are no longer under his yoke; but while he and they live, they have a claim upon him from which he is never completely absolved.

Surely it must be religion which prompts the Latter-day Saints to incur such serious responsibilities at the risk of being pronounced felons, and being stripped of property and citizenship by being incarcerated in the penitentiary.

Emmeline B. Wells, in a letter to the Women's Great Mass Meeting, writes:

That greater liberty has been given to women in our Church than elsewhere is indeed true; that now equality of sex prevails is undeniable. That men and women have always voted equally upon all ecclesiastical matters is a well-known fact, and the utmost freedom of speech has been the right and privilege of women in the Church from the first. That all this has been elevating in its tendency, and educational to woman, every careful observer must readily perceive. The aim and object of our institutions has been to lift women up to a higher standard of thought and intelligence, to protect and guard virtue, to promote self-reliance and individual development; and it is a privilege of our religion to teach our girls, as well as our boys, self-protection, and to instruct our boys, as well as our girls, that virtue and chastity are just as essential in man as in woman.

Mrs. Marilla M. Daniels, in her speech on that occasion, said:

We desire to express our indignation against the insults that are offered to our sisters that are brought before the courts and grand juries, and made to answer indecent questions or be fined and imprisoned for contempt. One is righteously indignant to think they will so far forget themselves and so dishonor their manhood as to insult defenceless women and children. Some of our sisters have been brought to untimely graves in consequence of such treatment; delicate and refined women have been made to suffer the keenest torture of mind through their insolence. What would they think if their wives, mothers, sisters, or daughters were treated in such a shameful manner? They seem to think they can insult a plural wife with impunity. There is in their estimation, no law to protect her; she has no rights.

Senator Edmunds once said that the very nature of every virtuous women revolted against polygamy and all its influences. There are thousands of my sisters in Utah and elsewhere who will bear me witness that this is not true of "Mormon polygamy." I can speak from a practical experience of over forty-one years. Our husbands, the fathers of our children, hold sacred their marriage covenants, and heaven's best blessings are a virtuous husband and good children. My father had born to him fifty-six children in the new and everlasting covenant. Many of them are now married, having families of their own, living in this and the adjoining Territories; and I venture to say they will compare favorably with any in the land for honesty, morality and integrity.   .

Whole pages could be filled with similar testimony from women who are the peers of our own mothers in every Christian grace and virtue, whose souls are unclouded by impurity and whose lives are fragrant with loving-kindness and good deeds; and despite the official utterances contained in congressional speeches and the President's message, I decline to join in the pharisaical prayer: "I am holier than thou!"

The recent official profession of faith on the sanctity of the legal marriage by the president, in his message, is a suggestive one. The solicitude of our [then] bachelor president for the sanctity of our homes, the regard for the mothers of our land, each "secure and happy in the exclusive love of the father of her children," (or compensated in a legal equivalent therefor), and the pride with which he argues that our best citizens are "the fathers of our families," are really touching. Inferentially we are informed that the man who is not surrounded in his single home with his wife and children, has no "stake in the country, respect for its laws, (or) courage for its defense."

A new convert is always superzealous. Though we can hardly assume that this profession of faith is to be considered in a Pickwickian sense, we must certainly regard it as official only; and as he stated, when last visiting Buffalo to vote, that he had left the president at Washington, we are warranted by both present logic and ancient history in considering it as the official belief of the president rather than that of the Buffalo bachelor.

On reading it I recalled my last visit to Utah. I spent several weeks in Southern Utah, but will recall here only one town, Provo, the largest south of Salt Lake City. Making myself comfortable under the hospitable care of my Mormon host of the Excelsior Hotel, I there, as in our Eastern villages, found the most enterprising of the citizens looked upon as the leading man, politically, morally, socially; leading and giving tone to "society." But there they called him Bishop instead of 'Squire. In Provo this individual was a Mr. S., who had lived there for years; been identified with its prosperity; had occupied high positions in the Territorial Legislature; had been one of a committee of three to codify the Territorial statutes, which were approved by Congress; had contributed freely to its institutions; had assisted to erect a fine opera house for the Provo Dramatic Club and visiting theatrical companies; had been particularly active in securing a really fine race track, where racing was *not* masked as an "Agricultural and Cattle Show;" besides assistance in building up home industries, etc. Provo contained from five to six thousand inhabitants, and Mr. S. was the peer of the 'Squires of our towns in every respect.

But I found that on his lot were three fine residences, and in each of them was a family calling him father. I was in a community where Mrs. Grundy threw no stones at this state of things; where plural marriage brought added social importance, to say nothing of the increased social standing, so to speak, as a wife of a patriarch in the Heavenly Zion; where every additional marriage can only be performed with the consent of the other wife, or wives; where children had grown to maturity, been tenderly and lovingly reared, their father and mothers respected, under a system where full as much loving care was bestowed on the guidance of youth as that displayed (officially) by Grover Cleveland.

One good old lady remarked to me: "Ah! it takes a sight of grace in a man to get on as harmoniously as they do with so many added cares." As I was a married man myself, I did not feel disposed to contest the point, for I knew I would be deficient in *grace*. "Parental care, authority and love," to all appearance, seemed to be regnant there.

I found in Mormondom no huge tenement houses, filled with families of overworked fathers, mothers, and children; no locality exhibiting the Avenue B side of civilization; no growing sons and daughters living and sleeping in a common family room, where the instincts of modesty are trampled upon under economic necessities, and vice proffers the bread which virtue denies. No, "these are not the homes of polygamy."

I found there no polygamic mothers, willing to barter their daughters' happiness, or wink at moral delinquencies, for the sake of ease; no mothers toiling for bare subsistence at starvation rates; no mothers forsaking their children to seek bread in prostitution. No, "these cheerless, crushed, and unwomanly mothers" were not the mothers of Utah.

I found there no polygamous fathers who never see their children awake on week days; no fathers doomed to a treadmill round of unremunerative toil, to whom every added birth added wrinkles to their brows; no fathers to whom children bring the expense of "hush money;" no fathers who look upon their children's coffins with that horrible complacency Christian civilization has instilled into the parental heart. No, "these are not the fathers of polygamous families."

Holding, as Mormons do, that cohabitation involves perpetual obligation, that the woman who gives her honor into a man's keeping has an endless claim upon him for support, and that plurality of wives, no more than plurality of children, requires a division of affection, they obstinately refuse to adopt the Eastern, and more civilized, plan in such cases made and provided by custom. Under the recent decision of Judge Zane a man may respect the law so far as to forego intercourse, yet if he recognizes the obligation solemnly covenanted, if he refuses to disavow the relation, turn her adrift, and brand their children as bastards, he is criminal.

Let me cite an instance. Geo. Q. Cannon had four wives, three of whom are still living. These women he married by mutual consent before the passage of the Edmunds law—1882—which made it a crime to live with more than one wife. He believes that he cannot in honor disavow connections nor restrict parental love for the children they have borne him to those Congress in its wisdom may select as alone legitimate. Yet he is a fugitive for this "crime" under the recent interpretation of the law. The late ex-Mayor Jennings once had two wives. The first died years ago; he remained content with the *ci-devant* No. 2. Though living in the single family relation for which our bachelor president had such (officially) unbounded admiration, both he and his wife were disfranchised.

Judge Zane's opinion has recently been officially promulgated by the United States, as henceforth the legally revised definition of "cohabitation." Thus, by a singular coincidence, Grover Cleveland becomes the official representative of the doctrine that "cohabitation" becomes "illicit" when you continue to support the mother of your "illegitimate" child under the alleged sanction of moral obligation. Consequently, to repudiate the mother and your covenants with her, and rear the child as a bastard, is now officially declared to be the straight and narrow way by which even a Mo,mon Elder may entertain reasonable hopes of entering into the gates of the White House.

In Utah, out of a population about three times greater than that of the State of Nevada enjoying home rule, there are twelve thousand disfranchised. But, as women are voters in Mormondom the population of "polygamous fathers" cannot exceed four thousand, and must be far less. Yet their children, their neighbors and friends, have made their cause their own and returned a unanimous Mormon Territorial Legislature. The anti-Mormons are not shrieking for individual or "minority rights," but to force their views on nine-tenths of the people. To the Mormon, government is a central authority two thousand miles away, and known only in the character of the men sent there, who are now fighting to keep their places. In Provo, a prominent court official loudly bewailed to me the benumbing influence of Mormonism in depreciating the sanctity of law, yet evincing his own disregard for law by swelling his legitimate income from the sale of drugs by the illegitimate sale of spirituous liquor to Mormon youth.

The president winds up his (official) declaration of faith that the safety of the country lies with the legal fathers by adding these words:

Since the people upholding polygamy are reinforced by immigration from other lands, I recommend that a law be passed to prevent the importation of Mormons into this country.

Shade of Jefferson! In view of these *facts*: 1, That every Mormon missionary goes out at his own expense, receiving no salary; 2, That plural marriage cannot be contracted till arrival in Utah; 3, That the converts are made in Christian lands among people taught to believe in the old-time sanctity of polygamous marriages, and that through their adherence to this creed, they rise from hopeless toil to independent farmers; 4, That polygamy is not obligatory, but a matter of mutual consent, the great majority not being polygamists and the male population being always in excess in Utah—in view of these facts, can a law be passed which does not aim at beliefs?

If we were going to embark in the preventive business and compel obedience to our views, we would modestly suggest that a law compelling fathers to marry the mothers of their children, rather than one offering a premium on disowning them, would be more creditable to the executive imagination, to say nothing of the Congressional conscience.

But, some one asks, " Then you indorse polygamy ?" Not at all.
I simply deny the moral right of law to enforce opinion, and, in this
case, against the protest of a whole people.   I deny the right of the
sixty thousand surplus females in Massachusetts, animated with the
virtuous indignation that ever influences the elderly maiden heart on
hearing that others enjoy "illicit cohabitation," to raise their shrill
voices and demand the extinction of those who are more fortunate
or unfortunate than they.

There is but one ray of hope which will meet the demands of
Law and Gospel.   Let them cast off the sense of obligation, or buy
the mothers off, let them adopt the customs in vogue in New York,
where fornication is not a crime: or imitate puritan Massachusetts,
where the "age of consent" is ten years; let them proclaim their
children bastards in the sight of the Lord and the Law, let them
abandon the women who trusted them to the operation of the almighty law of demand and supply,—and we warrant that the nation
will hear no more recommendations from the President "for such
further discreet legislation as will rid the country of this blot upon
its fair fame."   The same sentiment moved Louis XIV. when he
repealed the Edict of Nantes to drive Protestants out from France,
where they offended the Catholic majority.   And yet a so-called
representative of Jeffersonian Democracy, two centuries later, has
not arisen above the cry of the crowd-made conscience, and would
pose as the (official) defender of the marriage relation.   He would
have a legal crusade in behalf of monogamy, because the crowd-
made conscience holds it alone to be right.   I am not willing to
enforce my belief on others, or indorse a new tyrannous edict to
not only imprison, or drive out, but to keep out, Mormons from a
country that has been poetically, not officially, called "the land of
the free and the home of the brave."

A decision of the Supreme Court has not always been held as
sacred by the people.   The Mormons in denouncing the tyrannical
character of our laws are but imitating the New England clergy who
once had their moral sense similarly outraged in the Dred Scott case.
If they have no longer any confidence in the corporation attorneys
who sit on the Supreme Bench, and regard it as a partisan body,
that loss of confidence will be found to date back to the Electoral
Commission of 1877.   This blow at popular esteem for the judicial
ermine came from the Court itself, and the Mormons can hardly
be deemed disloyal for sharing a feeling that later judges in Labor
matters have made common to the entire country.   Some men are
so constituted that they cannot mingle with even refined ladies with-

out having their low natures excited by erotic desires; but shame, eternal shame, on the clergymen who, imitating the moral outlaws of our cities, invariably associate Mormon wives and Mormon homes with the thought of prostitution and promiscuity.

Four years ago I concluded my " Utah and its People " with words that the rapid progress toward centralization of power render more and more pertinent and impressive. They were as follows:

Polygamy in Utah is the consecration under religious obligation of the sexual relations, yet the Edmunds act assumes that it is identical with bigamy, or the betrayal and desertion of a woman through false pretenses!

This act not only brands men as criminal for following out their connections, in which woman's consent is a pre-requisite, but disfranchises even those who contracted plural marriage *before* Congress declared it to be a crime.

But in what does their crime consist? It is time to cease indulging in mere assumption, in appeals to passion and religious bigotry. In New York there is no law on the statute-book defining *fornication* as a crime, and all our pulpits are silent! You may, if unmarried, enter into sexual relations with a dozen women, so long as you do not represent them to be wives. Call them your harlots, your concubines, anything but wife, and you are guilty of no criminality.

Would it follow that if the miserable fanatic, the Mormon, could be induced to strike down the sacramental relation in which he holds marriage, if he should cease to give guarantees to both the woman and society, to stand by the results of this relation, he would be less open to clerical rebuke? If he adopted the suggestion of the Salt Lake *Tribune*, and recognized prostitutes as social missionaries, basing his sexual relations merely on animal passion, following New York rather than Biblical precedents, and lived in open and admitted fornication, there would be no law especially drafted to meet his case, the pulpit would be estopped from censure, and Christian society compelled to look elsewhere for its sacrificial goat!

If polygamy be barbarism, our superior civilization will crush it out. But right or wrong, be careful how you deny to even a " deluded " people the right of self-government, brand their children bastards, and turn them over for relief to the sense of equity possessed by a board of politicians. We tolerate the Shakers in seeking to prohibit and prevent marriage—certainly necessary to social existence. Let us endeavor to tolerate the men who regulate marriage on a religious belief, and who invariably discountenance and condemn every plural marriage by an apostate as wanting in that consecration which can alone sanctify. A crusade against those who refuse to recognize civil marriage, as the Catholic, is full as legitimate, and would be attempted, were their property centralized in a Territory.

We have learned to tolerate the religious heretic—in law, at least—but not the *social heretic*, and the Mormon problem brings before us a test which will try our boasted liberality to the utmost. When we, as a people, go two thousand miles to deny the right of self-government, because the *letter*, not the *spirit*, of law permits it; when we deprive citizens of the rights of franchise for acts of which those interested do not complain, but indorse, and which involves no moral criminality; when we do this to a people upon whose moral character the only blot is in the non-Mormon portion, we strike a blow at the American idea of liberty and toleration that might well arouse Thomas Jefferson from his tomb.

Whatever we may *think* of polygamy as a social system, let us be careful how we *act*, and not *fashion a handle for an axe which may one day strike nearer home when wielded by other passions.* Are there none of our statesmen who can rise above the fogs of prejudice and see the danger coercive measures must lead to? If moralists choose to ignore the Golden Rule, a statesman should not be blind to the peril involved in following a course mapped out by a few political adventurers in Utah. Leave to clergymen the honor of glorying over the possible apostacy of a few thousand Mormons from a faith which has kept them from profligacy and vice, or in their emancipation from moral control, and view the subject in a far broader sense. The Mormons point to the prophecy of Joseph Smith, that the time was not far distant when they alone would be the defenders of the great principle of religious liberty; shall the fulfillment of this prophecy come through the act of the representatives of a Republic founded by Jefferson and his colleagues?

If the Mormon home is not the childless home of the Eastern capitalist, nor the home of the factory operative, in which the belt of the mill connects with the cradle and weaves human lives into manufactured fabric, it is none the less a *home* consecrated by family love and sanctified by religious observances, where the mother's devotion guides the feet of loving children.

You know the Golden Rule, apply it in this case, or answer why not!

CHAPTER VI.

THE MORAL CRUSADERS.

THE theory of republican government is that it is with and by the consent of the governed. The *practice*, as prevailing in the Territories, is to govern without the consent of the governed, where certain social heretics are not even tolerated, their lives only being spared; and where loyalty is supposed to consist in open denunciation of men who furnish nearly all of the taxes and comparatively none of crime.

On the other hand we have seen that the alleged " theocracy " has mortally offended our tradesmen—as true to the instincts of his class to-day in America, as was his more ancient Pharasaic brother in Jerusalem—by inaugurating co-operation in both production and distribution; has revolted the tender consciences of the lawyers in Congress as well as out—unable to see beyond the text of what is written as ever were their Levitic prototypes—in dispensing with legal fees and their inestimable privilege of fomenting social discord; has shocked the moral sense of our great army of theologasters by requiring every member of the " priesthood," from the President down to the humblest Deacon, to labor for a living; and have blasted the hopes of political barnacles and sycophants by forbidding any man to hold office in its ecclesiastical organization without the consent and expressed approval of those among whom and for whom he is to exercise the functions of his office.

Could difference be more radical? The government, located twenty-five hundred miles distant, encroaching upon monarchical privileges, appoints the refuse of political conventions, or defeated candidates who have failed to secure support at home, without reference to the feelings or wishes of those to be governed. The " Theocracy," in precept and practice, making general acceptance so prominent a feature that no Mormon could be found mean enough to solicit an appointment to exercise authority over an unwilling people; where even the thearchs have no right to foist themselves or others into any position of honor or profit.

What the Mormons are we have seen; let us now glance at the

character of some of the past officials dumped upon Utah, and the acts of some of the present incumbents.

I have before me a circular issued in May, 1877, and signed by *A. Milton Musser*, "*Mormon*" *Elder*, a gentleman whom I have reason to know to be the peer in moral character and general attainments of any man in Utah of my acquaintance, and worthy of recognition in any assemblage of ladies and gentlemen as in every respect an honorable and truthful man. He said:

The red hot feeling now kindled against us is entirely unwarranted. I speak from the record, having been identified with the "Mormons" since 1846. I *know* that the excitement and consequent prejudice periodically fanned to blood heat against our citizens is made to promote the personal interests of very bad men. We have had, and now have in Utah, such frauds as Eliza Pinkston, J. Madison Wells, and Returning Boards by the score. To prove this I need but state that out of the appointments made by ex-President Grant, during the eight years of his incumbency, to places of trust in Utah, he was obliged to remove *forty-five* of them because of their dishonest, unlawful and rascally acts. These recalls were Governors, Acting-Governors, Secretaries, Judges, Land-Officers, District Attorneys, Marshalls, Special Mail Agents, and the like.

Let us glance at some of the "petty vices" of these official regenerators of Mormondom. The Judge through whose misrepresentation President Buchanan was induced to send an Army to Utah, leaving his wife and children behind him, brought a courtesan with him west, who sat by his side on the judicial bench! Another official, soon after his arrival, made improper advances to a respectable lady, whose sons, it was said, overtook him in his flight to the East, and for the gross insult to their mother deprived him of virility. Another, who received the appointment of Governor, with his son became the joint father of a waif, whose sorrowing mother on oath could not say whether the Governor was father or grandfather! Another Governor was not long there till he was discovered in a drunken debauch with an imported harlot, both of whom were in a state of primitive nudity! Still another—who was so greatly exercised at the Mormons because of their religious marriages that he never lost an opportunity to denounce them—was so incautious as to permit the embarrassing discovery of *hair pins* in his bed while his wife was thousands of miles away; a discovery which so digusted his Gentile hostess that she quitted the place without notice.

Again, another with his carpet-bag arrived to overshadow Utah with his stately presence. He was a leader in a bible-class on Sundays. Week days he varied the duties of his position by stump speeches in mining camps against the vileness of plural marriage. For unlawful and questionable acts his gubernatorial career came to a sudden end. The Utah report says: "On the way to the Pacific slope this spotless anti-'Mormon' scripture reader for a whole night contested the right of possession to a sleeping berth on a Pullman car with a woman not his wife, and neither being willing to surrender to the other, a joint occupancy was maintained the entire night."

Another, afterward convicted of malfeasance in office and removed, incited the only election riot Utah had ever know while grossly intoxicated, but produced the Governor to give sworn testimony that he was sober, when it was a matter of common notoriety on the streets that if sober it was an abnormal condition.

Without extending the list to an unnecessary length, I ask attention to the following extract:

We once had a judicial luminary that would not keep in his family's employ a servant-girl or washerwoman except on special personal considerations. Some years ago his wife and other ladies, of the same faith, sent East a piteous petition to the lady members of the same church for a Christmas gift of five dollars each, for the erection of a church in Salt Lake City, looking to the "amelioration of the Mormon women." Soon after the petition was made public one of the principle "lady" singers was fined for keeping a house of prostitution.

Many of our past officials have in every possible manner, by their judicial, official, and other acts, encouraged and screened prostitution and drunkenness. The pimp, harlot and rum-seller would draw on them at sight, and they were ever ready to honor their drafts and aid in crippling the local officers of Salt Lake City, and other places, with writs, injunctions, etc. Once upon a time a "Mormon" was sent to the penitentiary for a term of years and fined $300 by a "mission" judge for openly maintaining two wives and their children. When the Supreme Court of the United States set aside his extrajudicial proceeding, and released the "Mormon," an officer and a harlot rode out in a carriage to open the prison door, and while *en route*, it is said, they maintained the relation of married people.

Among the most ardent, but pitiable, would-be regenerators was a man whose ambition centred in subjugating the "Mormons," freeing Ireland from British rule, drinking whiskey, and making love to a subaltern's wife; while his own wife and children were off on a visit, he took as kindly to the proxy as measles takes to children.

The god-fathers of the anti-polygamy bill—a once highly respected government official, now an humbled citizen of Indiana; a man of New York City who free-loved his neighbors' wife and was shot by the outraged husband; and a would-be popular actress—all bitter enemies to our day-light, healthy and beautiful children-increasing marriages—have gone and are going into ineffable disgrace.

The story about one of Utah's carpet-bag anti-Mormon Judges selling out his unexpired term of office, with its "good will," to a fellow of his own stamp, for $2700, must be fresh in the minds of many. The buyer gave his note for the sum, which is not yet paid, notwithstanding his reported large special income, while on the judicial bench, from those interested in valuable mines. He too was one of the illustrious *forty-five* fire-eating, anti-"Mormons," General Grant was forced to cut out of Utah's official circuit.

* * * * * * * * * * *

This list is already offensively long. Money could not have tempted me to give so much publicity to such doggerels of humanity, but for their persistent, shameless and vile attempts to blacken the character of the unoffending people of Utah, by using their official positions and patronage to cover us with wide-spread and bitter . odium, so as to justify their mobbing us from our mountain homes, which we have so dearly earned at a cost of many millions of dollars and thousands of lives. This is my only apology for obtruding these *facts*—*facts* which are notoriously true in the great West, and which are tacitly *confirmed by their removal from office* by the general government for their villainous practices. I might add a painful list of cases where gamblers, rum-sellers, thieves, renegades, lechers and harlots have been habeas-corpused, and the local civil authorities enjoined by "Mission" judges, and others holding carpet-bag Commissions.

Nor has the gubernatorial record in late years been a savory one. The Mormons under the rule of Gov. Murray have again been nauseated with the usual scandals. They have seen his carriage followed in a Fourth of July procession by that of a woman of notorious moral profligacy, without protest, and have seen him intoxicated on the streets, the associate of sporting men and gamblers. They have watched his wild-cat mining business, as President of a Company that never owned a dollar's worth of property, but which needed a "live" man to unload its stock. Last year he prevailed upon the President to send troops to Salt Lake, just before Congress met, to influence public opinion against the Mormons and secure his own retention in office. But it having been demonstrated that no thought of resistance was entertained, that the only plot existed in the fertile imagination of the mendacious Eli, and his high-handed and arbitrary proceedings having left the Territory deficient in means to meet many current expenses, Mr. Cleveland has been forced to apply the official boot, and send him to join the grand army of his libidinous predecessors.

In the judicial proceedings against "illegal cohabitation" there are certain features which deserve attention of every thoughtful man who would not have prosecution identified with persecution. The third section of the Edmunds' law reads as follows:

That if any male person, in a Territory or other place over which the United States has exclusive jurisdiction, hereafter cohabits with more than one woman, he shall be deemed guilty of a misdemeanor; and on conviction thereof shall be punished by a fine of not more than $300, or by imprisonment for not more than six months, or by both said punishments, in the discretion of the court.

At first blush this would seem to be intended by our virtuous law-makers to strike at unlawful cohabitation *in any form*, whether practiced by Mormon or Gentile, in a western Territory or in the District of Columbia. But, bless your innocent heart, whatever may have been the intention of the legislators, the judiciary stood ready with a convenient definition. The first move was in the form of oath prescribed by the so-called Utah Commission, appointed under the Edmunds' law, and required to be taken by legal voters before they could register or vote, in which occur these words:

That I have not violated the laws of the United States prohibiting bigamy or polygamy; that I do not live or cohabit with more than one woman *in the marriage relation.*"

Consequently cohabitation *outside* of the marriage relation did not disqualify anyone. Every pimp was admitted into full civil fellowship with the most saintly Gentile. The churches and slums rejoiced together, victory was theirs. But lo! when the election returns were received, it appeared that while all polygamists were debarred from voting or holding office, the Legislature were all Mormons. The Utah Commission, in their report for 1884, are compelled to make the following admission:

Three fourths or more of the Mormon adults, male and female, have never entered into the polygamic relation, yet *every* orthodox Mormon, *every* member " in good standing " in the church, believes in polygamy as a divine revelation. *This article of faith is as much an essential and substantial part of their creed* as their belief in baptism, repentance for the forgiveness of sins, and the like.

Consequently it became difficult to secure witnesses, and in fact there have been but very few convictions under the act for polygamy. Many Mormons determined to obey the law relating to cohabitation, and lived henceforth with one wife only. But *law*, the " sanctity of law," must be enforced even if it were necessary to give a new meaning to the words used in the act. The court not only held that the intent of the act was solely to reach the Mormons, but **they** gave a new definition of the word "cohabit." Judge Zane, in the Angus M. Cannon case, gave the following decision, which has since been confirmed by the Supreme Court, namely:

I am of the opinion that it is not essential to constitute an offence against this law, to show sexual intercourse. It is sufficient to show that a man lives with more than one woman, cohabits with them, and holds them out to the world as his wives. That being so, that he did not have sexual intercourse with them, or occupy the same bed with *either* of them, is no defense and is immaterial, so far as the jury is concerned.

Under this ruling all evidence as to abstinence from cohabitation in the common, or "vulgar," not legal, acceptation was excluded. In his charge to the jury the Judge again laid down the law in these words:

If you believe from the evidence * * * that he *held them out* to the world by his language *or conduct*, or by both, as his wives, you should find him guilty. It is not necessary that the evidence should show that the defendant and these women, or *either* of them, occupied the same bed with the defendant, or slept in the same room. Neither is it necessary that the evidence should show that, within the times mentioned in the indictment, he had sexual intercourse with either of them."

Hence the criminality of cohabitation, in Utah, is by refusal to deny, or even by conduct to give rise to "reasonable belief" in the minds of bitter, unreasoning partisans, that they may be married. And for this end an army of sneaks and informers, with authority of inquisitors to intrude into the privacy of domestic relations with indecent questionings of children and women, becomes a necessity to maintain the "sanctity of law!" If a man "holds out" a woman as one with whom he has entered into solemn covenants not to abandon, even though he remains practically a stranger to her sight; or if he supports a woman in a distant county or territory, and thus gives rise to the suspicion of the horde of spotters, ever eager to pry into the affairs of their neighbors with prurient curiosity that there must be a plural marriage concealed in the relation, he is at once indicted and sentenced for unlawful cohabitation! But if a man has unlawful intercourse, even continuously, with any number of women, then, so long as he does not "hold them out" to the world as his wives, he is not guilty of unlawful cohabitation.

To "protect society," a man who has entered into solemn marriage obligations to protect the women with whom, as wives, he may have sexual relations, is sent to prison; while he who practices gross immoralities, yet abstains from specific pledges, goes free! To "protect society," a premium is placed upon the abrogation of sacred *contracts*, under a law that the courts admit was not enacted " in the interests of morality!" To " protect society " District Attorney Dickson said: " It was a matter of history that the Mormons did not cohabit together without a form of marriage, and it was *alone this form of marriage* and the practice under it, and *not sexual sins*, that Congress was legislating against! To " protect society " an American Jeffries abrogates a Mormon's right to " an impartial jury " by so ruling that the jury is packed to convict; officially announces that the object of the law is to remove such examples, " to compel them to *put away* their wives, to " cause a breaking up of their family relationships " ! Finally, to " protect society," young women are plied with indecent questions by profane deputies, or pulled from their beds in their night-clothes " to see if there was a man there;" a system of terrorism inaugurated; women arrested upon suspicion of being pregnant, and haled before a grand jury of anti-Mormon men to be plied with prurient inquiries into details, and children made to understand subjects beyond their tender years! Paraphrasing Madame Roland's famous apostrophe, we may well exclaim—"O Society, Society, what crimes are perpetrated in thy name"—by law!

It is a matter of record,—as in the Ames case,—that a man having seduced his wife's sister and a child being the result, was arrested on the complaint of his victim and bound over by a U. S. Commissioner to await the action of the grand jury, upon a charge of unlawful cohabitation, but being unable to furnish bail was committed to prison—he being a non-Mormon was taken by habeas corpus from the custody of the U. S. Marshal and discharged, the federal Chief Justice holding that the few acts of sexual intercourse in private, in the absence of " public repute " of holding out the victim as his wife, did not constitute unlawful cohabitation.

Per contra, it is a matter of record—as in the case of Lucy Devereux, a Mormon—that a young woman has been sent to the penitentiary for refusing to answer these questions:

1. Is not your little girl's name Mulzeta Maud Newsom?
2. Who is the father of your little girl?
3. Is not Wm. D. Newsom the father of your little girl?
4. After you went to live at Newsom's house did you not occupy the same bed with him?

The only hypothesis upon which the questions can be insisted upon is that the answers might lead toward proof of a marriage, for

her character *as a Mormon* prevented all other suspicion, or to unlawful cohabitation according to the "holding-out" theory. Why
should such evidence be ignored in the Ames case, and sought
with vindictive oppressiveness in that of Newsom, and the lady compelled to answer questions which would not be tolerated here by any
justice of the peace?

It is a matter of record—as in the Musser case and many others
—that jurors of admitted licentious habits have been accepted,
and conviction secured for acts committed *before* the passage of the
Edmunds' act. All the evidence showing the act to have been *ex
post facto*, it was held to be sufficient to establish the "general
repute" of "holding out," and the prisoners were convicted accord-
ingly. Again, when asked by Mr. Musser for instructions *how* to so
live as not be subject to punishment, Judge Zane replied:

You may live with either one, as you choose, providing that
you live with her as your wife, even though she might not be your
lawful wife.

But for his manly refusal to repudiate the others, though he did
not *live* with them, as we understand the word, he was convicted. Is
it a wonder that the Mormons compare such Judges to the vindicator
of the "sanctity of law" who once sat upon a bench in Babylon
and sentenced three Hebrew youths for "holding out" against the
idolatrous customs of their contemporaries?

It is a matter of record that the Mormons have been disfranchised in Idaho *en masse*. Governor Bunn, in approving an act
prescribing a test oath specially designed to exclude all believers in
the Mormon religion, says expressly, "The Mormons must either
purify their organization or cease taking part in the affairs of the
government;" while a Judge in Arizona, Howard, states that it requires but little law and less evidence to convict a Mormon.

Fred Dubois, U. S. Marshal of Idaho, previous to the trial of a
number of Mormons at Blackfoot, made the following startling
declaration: "I have now got a jury that will convict every Mormon brought before it on a charge of unlawful cohabitation, *innocent*
or *guilty*. It would convict Jesus Christ Himself if He were brought
into court on that charge." Subsequently Marshal Dubois was
subpœnaed as a witness in an unlawful cohabitation case, and being
placed on the stand, was asked by the attorney for the defendant to
state whether he had made the remark alluded to. After a moment's
hesitation he said: "Well, I guess I did say so."

It is a matter of record that a United States officer, Deputy Marshal Vandercook, and others, having been arrested, tried and convicted of "lewd and lascivious conduct," upon the evidence of eye-witnesses to the acts alleged, have been released under habeas corpus by Judge Zane. The accused, including an ex-United States Commissioner, ex-Assistant U. S. District Attorney and others, although convicted upon positive evidence, were acquitted by Chief Justice Zane upon appeal. He said that the city ordinance was valid, but then proceded to destroy its force by declaring that acts to be punishable must be committed publicly, and, inferentially, that the grossest lewdness can be carried on under the guise of privacy. To not misrepresent we quote from the decision. The Judge said:

The word indecent was substantially the same as lewd. It did not refer to single acts, but to a repetition of acts, openly and publicly scandalous. It did not have reference to private acts. * * * If an act were committed before the public, it offended decency; but if in private, it had no such effect. * * * The defendant is discharged.

It is a matter of record that the man who was chiefly instrumental in bringing these lecherous officials to trial—B. Y. Hampton—was indicted and convicted of conspiracy, although the truth of the charges was not denied but fully sustained; and that, further, in view of the imminent peril conviction would bring upon other moral crusaders against the Mormons, the clergy of the city, with the exception of the Catholic, united in a vigorous denunciation of the "conspiracy on the part of the Mormon officials" to collect reliable evidence "to blacken the character of public men. The attack on Christian ministers has begun." *O tempora ! O mores !* They thus not only cried out before they were implicated, but threw their clerical robes over men concerning whose *moral* crime there was no rebutting evidence !

It is a matter of record—as in the Dean case, April 27, 1886, and others—that the first and legal wife has been compelled to testify against her husband unwillingly in order to secure conviction. And again—as in the White case, May 17, 1886—a legal and only wife is compelled to give evidence against her husband to convict him of cohabitation with another wife who died before the indictment was found.

It is a matter of record—as in the Royal B. Young case and others —that although the evidence showed the relation to have been purely platonic by mutual agreement from the date of marriage, yet the indictments were made cumulative, and the victim convicted on several counts for the same offense, and sentenced to the full term

of six months and full fine on each count. To quote the charge
of Judge Power:

The offense of cohabitation is complete when a man, *to all
outward appearance*, is living or associating with more than one
woman as his wife. An indictment may be found against a man
guilty of "cohabitation," *for every day*, or other distinct interval of
time, during wnich he offends. Each day that a man cohabits with
more than one woman, *as I have defined the word cohabit*, is a distinct
and separate violation of the law, and is liable to punishment for
each separate offense.

It is a matter of record—as in the case of Apostle Lorenzo Snow
—a man may be arrested and convicted of "cohabiting" with his
wives, some of whom he had not seen since the Edmunds' act went
into effect, and convicted in the absence of all evidence, save that he
was "a leader of leaders." In fact, the judge seemed in his charge
to hold Mr. Snow culpable for not living in cohabitation; and this
gray-haired man, past the three-score-and-ten allotted to man,
with wives long since past child-bearing, is sentenced to eighteen
months' imprisonment upon three indictments, and convictions for
virtually the same offense—"holding out!"

If Lorenzo Snow, "a leader of leaders," could be sentenced for
having strictly followed the advice of the Court given to Mr. Musser,
to live with only one woman as his wife, what mercy could be expected for Presidents Taylor and Cannon? Mr. Cannon's well-
known sterling integrity and executive ability rendered him to the
crusaders a dangerous man to be at large. Mr. Cannon's long re-
sidence in Washington as Territorial Representative in Congress,
has made his name and figure familiar to many in the East. The
writer lived in Washington for several years and personally knows.
that Mr. Cannon stood above reproach in all that constitutes
character. A charge of misdemeanor was brought against him, and
a reward of five hundred dollars was set upon his head. He was
arrested while absent on a mission, and great was the glee mani-
fested over the fact. Although the alleged evidence rested upon the
slenderest authority, he was placed under the extraordinary bond of
$25,000; two other charges being trumped up against him, he was
held in $10,000 each, making the enormous sum of $45,000 for
what Congress had declared to be punishable by imprisonment not
exceeding six months or by a fine of not more than $300! Witnesses
were arrested on the Sabbath day and held in bonds varying from
$2,500 to $5,000. Every attempt was made to fasten upon him as
many charges as could be scraped up with the avowed intention

through segregated cohabitation cases to wear him out, ruin him in person, property and influence, and boasts freely made that he was to be sent to an Eastern prison under an accumulation of sentences which would be equivalent to imprisonment for life.

When juries are carefully selected from among Mormon enemies; when the law is so interpreted that "general repute" becomes evidence of criminality; when the demand of the Prosecuting Attorney is invariably echoed by a pliant Judge as a decision; when the well-known animus of the officials to "cage Cannon" is taken into consideration; when the Prosecuting Attorney is said to have openly asserted to his friends that indictments would be found enough to confine the prisoner for thirty years, and that he would be dead before the time was out; when indictment is equivalent to conviction, and grand jurors who have refused to bring indictments for segregated cases of the same offence have been sternly lectured from the befouled bench and discharged; what reasonable ground has any man to believe that Mr. Cannon could secure "a free and impartial trial by jury?"

That Mr. Cannon forfeited his bail bonds under such circumstances is not a matter of surprise; and the only surprise in the matter would be to find a single individual, Mormon or Gentile, where he is known, who would believe for a moment that his bondsmen would thereby be left pecuniarily in the lurch. George Q. Cannon had been marked for a prey to the "majesty of law," his very virtues making him a more shining mark.

What the Judges are before whom he was to appear we have seen. What the Prosecuting Attorney is, unfortunately, is a matter only too well known to the people of Utah. They have known him seek to force to immediate trial an invalid wounded and seriously sick; to shut a lady up in a room with a debauched deputy, to be insulted at his mercy; to compel virtuous mothers and maidens to appear before a grand jury to be plied with indecent questions which would call a blush to the cheek of any honorable man; to question young girls under the age of puberty concerning their own parents; to stand as the guard and legal bulwark of "private" licentiousness while honorable men, who refuse to "hold out" women, who have trusted them, as prostitutes and their children as bastards, are sent to prison with thieves and murderers.

Almost every charge brought by the colonies against the crown in our Declaration of Independence can be paralleled in Utah against the federal government. Judges as unjust as Jeffries befoul its

bench, and a vigor as vindictive as was displayed toward the Huguenots of France by the courts of Louis XIV., or by the courts of
Henry VIII. and Elizabeth toward Catholics, prevails in Utah.   As
I have stated polygamy is not the issue—that is but the illusory cry
of a host of lecherous and speculating adventurers hungry for the
spoils they anticipate when the Mormons are worn out, and the fruit
of their industry and thrift falls into their grasping hands.   Louis
XIV., Henry VIII. and Elizabeth, like the Roman Emperors before them, had an eye single to the "majesty of law."   The requirements of the State have sanctioned every persecution, whether
of the religious heretic who denied the faith of his rulers, the political heretic who denied the sanctity of the crown, or, as now, the social
heretic who denies the validity of the dictates of Mrs. Grundy in
both religious and economic matters.   In the Special Report of the
Utah Commission for 1884, we find a short passage which reveals the
source of bitterness on the part of the small minority who alone can
act as jurors on these cases.   Listen:

Nearly all of the agricultural land is already occupied, and it is
very evident that Utah can never support a large population.   The
present population is estimated at 160,000, about four-fifths
being Mormons.   The people are generally engaged in agricultural
pursuits, chiefly in a small way, relying mainly on irrigation.   Prior
to the completion of the trans-continental railway through Utah in
1869, there were very few non-Mormons in the Territory.   Since
that time the business of mining has become an important interest,
several of the most valuable mines of silver and lead in the
West being located there.   Besides, there are some gold mines and
valuable deposits of coal, iron, copper, and other minerals.   The
mines give good employment to a great many persons, and have
been the means of attracting a considerable *non-Mormon population.*
Many of the non-Mormons (or Gentiles) are doing a prosperous
business in banking, mining and *mercantile pursuits.*   Candor requires
us also to say that personal security and property rights appear to
be as inviolate in Utah as in any of the States or Territories.   However, business men of small capital, *among the Gentiles,* complain ot
dull times by reason of the clannishness of the Mormons in trading
with each other rather than with the Gentiles.

That bankers, miners and merchants should violently complain
of dull times in a community based on co-operation as a fundamental
principle, need not astonish us, neither does the fact that Mormons
prefer trading with each other in preference to their traducers.   Cor-
porationt, and the individual merchant buying in the cheapest
market and selling in the dearest, have struck hands in Utah against

the social heretics who retard their avaricious rush for gain by eliminating the selfish factor, in a great measure, from their social system. Whatever may be the *conscience* of the mining speculator, the banker computing usury, or the tradesman haggling over his wares; whatever may be the *conviction* of the official and unofficial lawyers educated to make the worst appear the better reason—for a fee—the conscience and conviction of an honest man must go out to the struggling people so cruelly assailed under the pressure of competition to secure legal privilege and advantage over one's fellows, the sole competition existing to-day in channels of trade.

With these apostles of the modern gospel of greed, willing to sacrifice anything for personal profit, we find arrayed the Protestant Church.

. The Church, as our spiritual guide, has grossly neglected her duties and wallowed in the mire of self interest; and, instead of exercising a spiritual power to overcome greed with nobler motives, she has struck hands with the disorganizing influence of selfishness, rewarding her shrewdest and most over-reaching members with the Church offices, until " deacon " has become a synonym for far other characteristics than once hallowed the word—conforming in their management to current "business principles," so that it may be said of every new church-building in process of erection that the love of gain on the one hand and human despair on the other, becomes incorporated between every layer of brick, or stone and mortar, until religion bids fair to become a hollow mockery, and its forms of worship but the ritual of a system where legally restricted competition has been deified as the savior of men, and the spirit of greed installed on the throne of the universe to give sanction to the fundamental principle of our Christian civilization: " Every man for himself and the devil take the hindmost!" Success in life has been set forth as consisting in the acquisition of wealth, in the mere accumulation of capital, even though only attainable through the failure of others less shrewd, and national prosperity is said to prevail where the more grasping and avaricious are easily enabled to climb over their fellows and escape from the slough where the great mass must remain, in no wise benefited but often cursed by the individual escapes. This is fast becoming the popular gospel, in fact may be said to be the religion of the State, and for which the State exists; and for its spread the selection of missionaries to extend its baneful influence in once peaceful Utah could not have been made more thoroughly capable of doing its dirty work.

Monogamy, like religion, requires no coercive policy for its preservation. If monogamy, and its constant shadow, prostitution, are indeed essential to the preservation of civilization, have no fears of toleration. The true remedy for the abuses of freedom, said Macaulay, is more freedom.

CHAPTER VII.

WHAT IS THE LABOR MOVEMENT?

THE struggle between the representatives of capital and labor is world-wide. All along the lines the din of strife is heard. In France, Decazeville and St. Quentin echo with the tread of strikers and troops. In Spain the workmen of Madrid flaunt their rags and demand employment, while their comrades of the rural districts, goaded to desperation, set fire to barns. Even Portugal awakens from its lethargy to witness the strange spectacle of imposing manifestations at various points against taxation, and at Oporto the workmen raised the ominous cry of " Long live the Republic ! " In Italy the peasants of the mountain districts are taking the administration of justice into their own hands and rendering the lives of the gentry insecure. In Russia new conspiracies are unearthed and new victims resignedly meet their fate. In Turkey, apparently buried in Asiatic lethargy, the street-sweepers of Constantinople astound the sleepy authorities by striking for their pay. In Germany the gory spectre of revolution is ever present before the statesman's mind. In England, the land of routine and commonplace, the great strikes in the North and the recent Socialistic mob in London makes even the optimist to pause.

In America, strikes and disorders form the current news of the day; from the Atlantic to the Pacific the air seems charged with an exhilarating ingredient which inspires men's thoughts with new purposes. Day by day the lines are being drawn closer and closer. Capital, alarmed, seeks to deny to labor the right of organization. Labor, feeling the strength of partial organization, takes on a new and independent tone. As passions are excited and temper aroused, wisdom too often is unheard while ignorance cryeth aloud. Compare the public feeling to-day with that of ten years ago, before the Pittsburgh riot startled the country from its dream of centennial grandeur and peace; we seem to have passed into a new age. These signs are but sporadic manifestations of the growing discontent. As in all pre-revolutionary days they are indications of a coming struggle, and yet men talk of an equitable adjustment of the strained relations between capital and labor through the use of force.

Any system requiring force to sustain itself, is already judged in advance.

In the opening years of the French Revolution all statesmen were seeking an equitable adjustment between authority and liberty, striving to attain a happy twilight medium between light and darkness which would yet give satisfaction to each. None sought a republic, yet almost before the ink on the adjusting protocol was dry, the republic was proclaimed. The logic of events always leads men; the process is never the reverse. In 1775 the Colonists sought an equitable adjustment of their differences with the crown. The boycott on tea was deemed an extreme step. Then came the Boston Massacre, and as the smoke rolled away over the land, independence was born. Again in 1861, thoughtful men were seeking a new compromise between antagonistic principles in order to preserve the Union. A shot was fired at the flag on Fort Sumter and the North became solid.

We are passing through similar scenes. The demands of the future are arrayed against the entrenched customs of the past. We are growing into a state where the arrogance of those who stand by the past and would repel progress, or the ignorance of those who while unconsciously representing the future are yet human in their passions, may precipitate a conflict which will stain the pages of the history of this century with the blood of slaughtered victims. As has been well said, compromises are incipient suicides. It behoves us to understand the fundamental principles involved in the conflict, for the contending forces in the seething crucible of social life are beyond men's control. What will be the outcome it were rash to say, but in what direction all the tendencies of progress lead is not a matter of prophecy.

Let us make the subject a personal one. You work for wages. Are they increasing? Is your position a guaranteed one, or is it dependent upon uncertain conditions and a fluctuating market? Are you to-day satisfied, or are you striving for something better? In short, it is a personal question. A very few years ago such questions would have been idle; to-day they find receptive ears. Is there not in this fact a pregnant meaning? Do you not realize that times have changed since our civil war, if your memory goes back beyond that event? You are a mechanic: Have you the opportunities now that there were then for the man of small means to start for himself? Is not the small manufacturer, the small trader being driven to the wall? Can the capital of a few hundred dollars compete with that of millions? Is not your daily routine becoming a fixed one? You feel the lines drawing yearly closer which hold you in the rut of wage labor; you realize more and more the lack of opportunity to escape by raising yourself above your fellows; you look ahead to old age and can see no relief unless it be a seat beside a son's or daughter's hearth to eat the crumb of dependence, while they are following the same weary round where your strength was worn out. On every hand you find gigantic changes going on in production, as in the startling fact that in the past fifteen years the whole power of mechanism in our country has doubled, having risen from 2,300,000 horse power in 1870, to 4,500,000 in 1885.

As an American, you of course read the papers. You read of strikes and lockouts; of suffering communities struggling for better remuneration. In your walks you meet with idle men who would work as gladly as yourself if the law of demand would permit, and you read with a pang the statement of the National Labor Commissioner that over one million men are in enforced idleness. You are familiar with the tenement-house quarters of our cities, perhaps necessarily so. You know its influence on health, on the morals of your children, on the happiness of your family circle. As an American, I ask you is this continued discontent the necessary outcome of our republican institutions? Is there virtue in the constitution to heal the existing antagonism between the representatives of capital and labor. Is there power in *political* legislation to remove the *economic* cause which compels you to bring up your children in a human bee-hive? Will the ballot restore the faded cheek of your wife or preserve the bloom of health on the faces of children doomed to factory toil? In other words how can political remedies secure economic results?

Let us weigh existing remedies before considering new ones. Was your father a wage-worker before you in this land of the free? Is your condition better than his was? If so, has it been acquired by reason of your political freedom? You may attend church. Whatever religion may have done for your moral nature, has it done aught for your economic condition, other than too often inculcating contentment and submission? Whatever may be the love and veneration you entertain for the church of your fathers for spiritual consolation, you know better than to look there for this relief. Is it not equally true that political freedom has done absolutely nothing to better your economic condition? You feel that neither the realm of religion nor politics intersect that of economy under our present industrial system.

You have mental freedom, but long years of conflict and blood-

shed were necessary to establish it. You fully recognize the *right*
of every one to the free use of his reason; that there can be no
greater blasphemy than the denial of freedom of thought; that what
was once deemed the sacred prerogative of God is now the treasured
right of self. In the realm of mental relations you deny coercive
authority and proclaim liberty. You also inherit political freedom.
Our fathers achieved it with their swords. It is a legacy of which
we are proud, nor would I undervalue it; nor, on the other hand,
should we overvalue it.

Mental freedom! political freedom! These are acquired. We
need not contend for these; they are ours. But economic freedom!
Ah! here we attain to a glimpse of the lines of progress. Since the
sixteenth century humanity has been tending to wider personal freedom. It is the trend of progress, and there has been a consequent
restriction of authority of man over man. Since then political questions have largely replaced religious ones in the governments of
the world until the present century. To the men of the seventeenth
century religious freedom seemed all that could be desired, and that
the line of progress henceforth must be towards its greater extension, by extorting new safeguards, establishing new guarantees. So
thought men; not so Humanity. Toleration once secured, the logic
of events would prevent reactive measures from being successful.
A principle once victorious, the standard is ever pushed on to new
fields of conflict.

The eighteenth century presented political questions for consideration, free, largely, from the religious phase in which they had
been clothed; questions not to be settled by religious methods.
Men read Junius, Rousseau, Paine. Political freedom was the spirit
of the age, and the great thinkers of the times were those who best
caught its meaning and translated into intelligent speech, rendering
explicit that which had been unconsciously implicit in the human
mind. Washington and Kosciusko in two continents gave it voice.
In France the beating hearts of men long used to repression felt a
new thrill. When the head of Louis XVI. rolled from the guillo-
tine, the descending blade severed the fiction of divine right to
govern. Could not force arrest the cause of progress? Could man
used to oppression dare to resist authority sanctified by "divine
right?" In vain! in vain! The advancing tide could not be
checked. The dykes were broken! The flood came and the empty
fiction was swept away. The people triumphed over authority because they gave voice to the spirit of the age. The fitting occasion
was offered and success attended the effort. The Bastile, that

sombre incarnation of authoritative Force, the visible symbol of the divine right of man to govern man, was destroyed.

July 14, 1789! It was the opening of a new era in the martyrdom of Man. "It is a revolt!" exclaimed the astonished monarch. "Sire," answered Lemoignon, "it is a revolution!"

Another century is nearing its close. Has it also a new spirit leading on to broader freedom? Has it a new Ideal, another standard than that of the past, seeking expression in action? Does it also contend with authority and force? If so the public questions which have characterized our century must attest it. Are they religious? Assuredly not. Are they political? Such we have thought them to be, but each year proves that they are more and far broader. The spirit of an age is ever the assertion of a great principle not yet attained. The living issue, the legitimate successor of its predecessors is Industrial Freedom. All the great questions of this century, since England began factory legislation in 1802, have been *economic*. Corn laws! Freedom of commerce! Tariff! Colonization! Strikes! Co-operation! All have the same inspiration in various degrees of intelligible articulation. The Chartists of England felt its breath when they stained the field of Peterloo with their blood. In 1830 it was faintly heard in the streets of Paris; in 1848 it moved the pulses of thousands and found audible voice. In 1871 its cry rang out and its flag was unfurled to shake the thrones of Europe. Drowned in blood it still serves to awaken a thrill in the breasts of millions—ominous prophecy of the future.

State patriotism is as obsolete as church creeds to move men to action. Nations still go to war, but it is now for a *market*. England and Russia contend for Midland Asia. France, Italy, Germany, Spain, all are seeking new colonial dependencies from economic reasons. It is a question of exports and imports. The productions of labor must find an outlet to new markets; foreign granaries must be secured to satisfy craving stomachs of workmen at home. Home producers cannot always buy that into which they have too often hammered or woven their lives. A foreign market must be sought, and won, by the sacrifice of other lives. The 110,585 boys and girls under thirteen years of age in England's textile factories may be ragged and pinched, but British fabrics must be exported to keep them in bread.

Two score years ago the tariff was a vital question in our land; to-day it is but a superficial one, of value only to political gamesters. To-day the desperate struggle of all European powers for a foreign market has rendered it a dead issue. Shall we protect, that is, endeavor to advance happiness, by curtailing freedom? Then we abandon foreign markets which our growing population increasingly demands and bend under " over-production." Shall we have free trade? Then Labor must fall to the universal level. In the one case we starve from the want of a market, in the other the same fate awaits us in the struggle for one!

Where then is the remedy? Politics offers none. Our political state is based on the present economic condition of things. The ballot can determine a choice of methods only; it cannot strike deeper. To do so would endanger vested interests, disturb proprietary rights, violate commercial contracts, jeopardize established institutions, unsettle law and order, peril religion itself! Still the cry of the age grows in distinctness; still angry men band together to secure shorter hours of toil, or to look on the gleaming bayonets of the militia on guard. The terrible struggle of States for economic advantage is the wrestle of despair to avert the inevitable doom statesmen foresee and dread. It is a death struggle where failure is inevitable to some. The politico-economic State has grown aged; it is in a moribund condition; only new methods can restore its arrested circulation. The hand of Progress has written the warning message upon the wall; the meaning of history attests its interpretation—wider freedom; mental, political, economic! In the living gospel of Progress we found our hope, in living Humanity we again behold Christ incarnate, and in its coming advent our future life. The old bottles answered to hold the old wine of politics, but are now bursting under the pressure of the new vintage.

We now see that the spirit of the age is not a new standard, a new Ideal, but the same one shifted from the field of political, to that of industrial relations. All questions resolve themselves on final analysis to the fundamental one: Liberty or Authority; freedom or force. And he who has a clear conception of the meaning of history will not hesitate to align himself on the side of the future rather than the past, with progress rather than with reaction. The living question of the present is that stated in the preamble of the constitution of the Knights of Labor as " the abolishment of the wage system," a problem the Mormon has alone solved.

If all present questions are, and have been, purely economic, in what sense was the late rebellion of the Southern States such? And as the question has a direct bearing on the Mormon problem it merits attention. A quarter of a century ago I enlisted in response to the call for troops. For three years I gave my services for the defence of my country. "Our liberties were at stake!" Could I hesitate? Young and ardent I looked forward to the time when my infant child should have become a school girl, a young woman, a wife and mother. While others would recall with pride that their fathers fought for national liberty, she should not hang her head speechless. It was the logic of patriotism. In response to its dictates I gladly served in defense of "the flag of the free!" To-day I view the graves of my comrades fallen with different emotions. Looking back over the score of years since I returned to enjoy a perpetual pension of water and air, the delusion has vanished. The question is *not* asked: "Did your father enlist?" Nay, more, my doubts extend further. I ask myself for what I fought? Liberty? Preservation of the Union? Or rather for the changes which every civil war entails; the enrichment of speculators ennobled by the patent of an army contract; or, taking advantage of national necessities, the manipulation of the money of the country for private ends; the centralization of authority, the tendency of industrial enterprise to concentrate into monopolies?

The fallen are honored—once a year. The survivors live to wonder at their past delusion. In preserving the Union we created a new union—of capital. Not that of legitimate capital with *free* competition and equal opportunities, but entrenched behind legal enactments and overriding competition through control of conditions. We enlarged the bounds of political freedom by embracing the emancipated freedmen as equals—in industrial bondage. Through the influence of the conqueror's sword the "freedmen" owe the economic change from the selling of the worker to the highest bidder to the selling of his work to the lowest bidder! We restored law and order with the bayonet, and made the fashion permanent.

The industrial system of the North, characterized by its *freedom* from all responsibility to labor, had been crossed in its path by slave labor in the territories. The cry of the North, the animating soul of its system, was that fierce struggle for precedence and advantage miscalled competition, and carries with it as a consequence cheap labor. Cheap labor brought business, commercial activity and the extension of modern civilization. The economic pressure behind was too great to admit of compromise. They were rival industrial systems which had met in the same path, and one must give way.

The war followed. The economic conditions of life suffered a violent change. A vast army had to be clothed and fed, and contractors found there a rich harvest. Great loans were necessary and speculation became inoculated into the fever of business life. The demand for labor increased, and lists of American wages were published in foreign lands by our consuls to induce immigration, lest dearness should check production. In this general industrial prosperity the farmer sought a share. Government was called in to aid in the extension of great highways of communication.

The dominating genius of the North—private greed—was incited by prodigal gifts of land as indemnity for capital advanced, and the people's heritage was quickly swallowed up. The South failed and reconstruction ensued. To-day, South and North alike admit the fundamental principle of our industrial system, the corner stone of our economic structure: *Free labor is cheaper than slave labor.* Employers without responsibilities could find new fields for enterprise when the system which entailed responsibilities was once removed. The South are converted; the poverty of a factory population is no longer an Eastern peculiarity. The gray meets blue in hearty unison to draw dividends and cut coupons. They have found free labor the *cheapest.* Wages still follow the old economic law, *the cost of subsistence,* and irresponsibility for sickness and old age follows freedom from employer to employee. Why should not the South have wept over Grant's bier?

The civil war had opened new paths to fortune, incited new passions, and found means to gratify them. The same changes which the conquest of Carthage and Greece introduced into the Roman Republic have been introduced here. We have had our Punic war and see it followed by reckless extravagance, profligacy, and an aristocracy of wealth. And it is for the further extension of this that the cry has gone forth that the Mormon must go!

O, trusting fetich-worshiper! have you a faith greater than that which can remove mountains, to believe that with your ballots you can reach and modify the economic laws underlying even the electoral system? Do you propose to vote down the growth of the limbs when you carefully water the roots? Can the ballot affect the amenities of social life, alter the laws of chemical affinity, abolish the correlation between wealth and power? But you say, if we hold together we may, by the ballot, limit the power of capital! So it has been said: "If fishes were gold, all would take to the water!"

Yet neither are true. In the later case, you would find on the banks of each stream the placard: "No Trespass!" In the former case, even admitting a possibility no whit more probable, you could only succeed in deranging economic conditions, withdrawing capital from enterprise, and introduce general distress and misery more keen than yet seen. Ballots might destroy or derange, but in whatever number cast could not give confidence. It is cheapness of means and prospect of profit that calls forth capital from its hidden coffers. The system and its methods are one. The issue is not how to reform abuses and retain cheapness. The nineteenth century is not called upon to discover how by ballot we may secure "a fair day's wage for a fair day's work" without striking at the tap-root of the tree where cheap labor is the life-giving sap. The question is a fundamental one, reaching below our whole social system, and is not to be solved by the application of surface emollients.

The Mormons have solved the problem for themselves and are offering a passive resistance to oppression. American workmen are banding together with similar economic motives to supplant our industrial system by one based on co-operation and arbitration. Will they, like the Mormons in their struggle, feel the weight of oppression? Time will tell. Both are unconsciously marching in the same direction; both have received the same inspiration.

From God to man the sceptre passed, but progress did not halt. The priestly amulet and the kingly crown no longer have mystic power in government. We calmly label them and hang them in our museums as curiosities. Under the economic conditions which the present century ushered in, the dream of our fathers has not been realized. The *purse* has succeeded the crown as the symbol of authority. In our efforts to secure, through thorough organization and passive resistance, the inauguration of a better system, wherein there will be a full and free co-operation and labor receive "a full, just share of the value or capital it has created," let us bear in mind the ties of industrial affiliation by which we are connected with the persecuted Mormons. The same spirit that is striving in the halls of Congress to devise new and more despotic measures to crush the Mormon industrial system, is also plainly visible in the recent decision of our courts in relation to boycotts. The Mormon is free to worship God *if* he will not endanger profits! We are free to organize *if* we will be content to remain home and suck our thumbs. The same rod which has lashed them, and which is now being fashioned into a more deadly club to break down co-operation and arbitration in Utah, is now being turned to the same end nearer home.

Any people who may be proven to rely on the great features of co-operation and arbitration as cardinal factors in their social system are, however, unconsciously our friends and allies. To-day Congress, so silent to petitions and demands of working men and women, easily finds time to draft new bills to crush the distant Mormon, to convert happy homes into scenes of discord, and extend commercial prosperity at the cost of the introduction of poverty and misery.

We have a right to insist that there shall be no more legislation in the nature of Coercion acts for Utah, until a full and fair investigation has been had by a competent Commission. Barren as may be the result of a thorough investigation at the hands of the politicians who could alone compose a Congressional Committee, even in their hands facts hitherto purposely concealed would be brought out, and the economic aspect of the problem brought into clearer relief. This at least we have a right to demand of the men we see fit to intrust with the responsibilities of our representation. In the meantime, while witnessing the growing aggressiveness of capital and its firmer hold acquired over legal processes, the shameless subserviency of the judiciary to its selfish interests, and the hearty alliance between the befouled bench and the political representatives of the people, we may gain a sterner resolve not to weaken in this struggle, the heir of the ages,—industrial independence.

If the facts I have given in the foregoing pages tend to awaken interest in the social system of the Mormons, if it incites a deeper interest in their attempt to solve the social problem of the age, and if above all it will lead a few to protest against condemnation and persecution before investigation, the writer will have accomplished his purpose.

In the present chapter I have made an attempt to outline the nature and significance of the so-called labor movement. How near it is akin to the Mormon question you will determine, as well as whether the signs of the times indicate the approach of a legal crusade in the East to bolster vested wrongs and to intrench injustice.

Shall we meet the blow with Mormon passiveness? However dissimilar the Mormon Saint and our workingmen, still underlying the social question which in reality constitutes the secret spring of antagonism to both, there is the spirit of the nineteenth century urging men on, the voice of the living future crying out against the voice of the dead past, living demands of the present arrayed against the entrenched privileges of the dead. Can the issue be doubtful?

Doth Progress halt as on revolve the ages
In man's sad martyrdom to power's behest?
Has Freedom yet no goal foreseen by sages,
No broader vision worthy earnest quest?
Did Progress cease when Luther's fight was ended,
Or when the king from his high throne descended,
Bequeathing heirs of want and sorrow blended—
The toiling millions—but a deafened ear?

Or is the dream that stirs our inmost being
To larger vision and clairvoyant seeing,
A phantom riddle e'er before us fleeing,
    Unanswered and unanswerable here ?

Blot out the thought ! vile offspring of man's greed
    That prates of peace when profits are in danger;
As long as toilers live in enforced need,
    Freedom unto their lives is e'er a stranger.
Freedom of thought ! It was a bold endeavor,
And millions fell ere mankind could dissever
The fatal bonds which held mankind forever
    Benumbed and lifeless in its iron grasp.
Yet onward in the van with exultation
Freedom, despite the bigot's lamentation,
Led freemen forth to further immolation,
    With blood-red hand to other laurels clasp.

When Capet's head rolled 'neath the scaffold's blade,
    And France redeemed rose from her nightmare slumber;
When Yankee patriots marched o'er hill and glade,
    That tyrants should no more our shores encumber—
Did we attain to Freedom's full fruition
In paving paths for partisan ambition,
While millions still lay bound in serf condition,
    The economic slaves of self and greed ?
Nay ! ballots bring to such no reparation,
Nor ease to bear the iron condemnation
That wages bring, condemned to degradation,
    To unrequited toil and life of need.

The battle is not o'er, the means of life
    From avaricious hands must yet be wrested;
The right to think and vote ends not the strife
    When right to bread in other hands is vested.
The priest has passed, his fatal bonds are riven,
The monarchs flee, by people's wrath out-driven,
And Church and State, to scheming traders given,
    In terror stand confronting Freedom's van.
The toiling millions see the bright day breaking,
The scheming few, in law entrenched, are quaking,
For Freedom dawns and strong men are awaking
    Resolved to end man's martyrdom to man !

www.ingramcontent.com/pod-product-compliance
Lightning Source LLC
Chambersburg PA
CBHW022013050726
47499CB00007BA/2561